THIS HAPPY BREED

BOOKS BY NOEL COWARD

Middle East Diary

THIS HAPPY BREED

A PLAY IN THREE ACTS BY

 Noel Coward

1947

DOUBLEDAY & COMPANY, INC.

GARDEN CITY, NEW YORK

TO HUGH BEAUMONT

CHARACTERS

FRANK GIBBONS

ETHEL, his wife

SYLVIA, his sister

VI

QUEENIE } his children

REG

MRS. FLINT, his mother-in-law

BOB MITCHELL

BILLY

SAM LEADBITTER

PHYLLIS BLAKE

EDIE

The action of the play passes in the dining-room of the Gibbons house, Number 17 Sycamore Road, Clapham Common

CONTENTS

ACT ONE

SCENE I

TIME

June, 1919.

SCENE

The scene is the dining-room of Number 17 Sycamore Road, Clapham Common. On the right as you look at it there is a fireplace. At the back a french window opening on to a narrow stretch of garden. On the left downstage is the door leading into the hall and through which, when open, can be seen the staircase.

The time is about eight-thirty in the evening, and, being June, it is still daylight. The french window is open and over the fence at the end of the garden can be seen a May tree in blossom.

The Gibbons family have only just moved in and so the room is chaotic. There are pale squares on the wallpaper where the last tenant's pictures hung; a huddle of odd furniture; several packing cases and odd parcels, etc. The only piece of furniture in position is a large sideboard which is against the wall on the left.

MRS. FLINT *is sitting in a cane armchair by the empty fireplace. She is a woman of sixty, soberly dressed in black. She has worn her best clothes for the move as she didn't fancy packing them.* ETHEL, *her daughter, a tall woman of*

15

*thirty-four, is bustling about arranging furniture and un-
doing parcels. She looks rather hot and untidy as it has been
a tiring day. From upstairs comes the sound of intermittent
hammering.*

MRS. F. (*querulously*)
What is Frank doing?

ETHEL
Putting up the curtains in the front bedroom.

MRS. F.
He'll have the house down in a minute.

ETHEL
They've got to be up before we go to bed tonight, we can't
have the whole neighbourhood watching us undress, can
we?

MRS. F.
They couldn't see right across the road.

ETHEL
Well, they've got to go up sometime.

MRS. F.
Nobody's thought to put any up in my room; there's no
blind either. I suppose I don't matter.

ETHEL
Oh, do shut up grumbling, Mother. You know perfectly well
the blinds haven't come yet and your room is at the back
anyhow.

MRS. F.
A nice thing if Mr. Whatsisname next door 'appens to go
out into the garden and looks up.

16

ETHEL

We'll send him a note asking him to keep his head down.

MRS. F.

It's all very fine to laugh.

ETHEL

I don't know what's the matter with you today, Mother, really I don't. Moving in's no picnic anyhow and it only makes things worse to keep complaining all the time.

MRS. F.

Me complain? I like that, I must say. I've 'ad a splitting headache ever since two o'clock and I 'aven't so much as mentioned it—rushing about here, there, and everywhere, and a fat lot of thanks I get.

ETHEL

It's all right, Mother, cheer up, you'll feel better when you've 'ad a nice cup of tea.

MRS. F.

If I ever *do* 'ave a nice cup of tea.

ETHEL

Well, the kettle's on, but Sylvia isn't back yet.

MRS. F. (*contemptuously*)

Sylvia!

ETHEL

She 'ad to go to the U.K. Stores, you know, and that's quite a way.

MRS. F.

She wouldn't 'ave 'ad to do that if she 'adn't forgotten half the things we told her to order. That girl's getting sillier and

17

sillier every breath she takes. I wouldn't be surprised if she
'adn't forgotten the number of the house and lost herself—
her and her anaemia!

ETHEL

Well, she can't help her anaemia, can she, now?

MRS. F.

I don't know how you and Frank put up with her, and that's
a fact.

ETHEL

Now you know as well as I do, Mother, I couldn't let my
own sister-in-law live all by herself, could I? Specially after
all she's been through.

MRS. F.

All she's been through, indeed.

ETHEL

I suppose you'll be saying next that she wasn't engaged to
Bertie and he wasn't killed, and they've lived 'appy ever
after!

MRS. F.

Sylvia 'asn't been through no more than anyone else has, not
so much if the truth were known. What she needs is a job of
work.

ETHEL

She couldn't stand it, she's too delicate; you know what the
doctor said.

MRS. F.

That doctor'd say anything. Look now he went on over
Queenie's whooping-cough, frightening us all to death.

18

ETHEL

Give us a hand with this little table. We can move it over by the window for the time being, it's not heavy.

MRS. F. (*rising reluctantly and helping with the table*)
I'm not supposed to lift anything at all, you know—not anything.

ETHEL

All right, all right, now you can 'ave a nice sit down again.

MRS. F. (*sitting again*)
This house smells a bit damp to me. I 'ope it isn't.

ETHEL

I don't see why it should be, it's not near any water.

MRS. F.

Well, you never know. Mrs. Willcox moved into that house in Leatherhead and before she'd been in it for three months she was in bed with rheumatic fever.

ETHEL

That's right, dear, look on the bright side.

MRS. F.

Isn't that the front door?

ETHEL

Yes. I gave Sylvia a key. She's probably lost it. I'll go and see.

MRS. F.

Perhaps she's been run over, and it's the police come to tell us.

(ETHEL *goes into the hall; after a moment she returns, followed by* SYLVIA, *a pale woman of thirty-four, carry-*

19

ing a large parcel of groceries which she plumps down on the sideboard with a sigh.)

Well, you've taken your time, I must say. We thought something 'ad 'appened to you.

SYLVIA

I'd like to see you be any quicker with a lot like that to carry. (*She groans.*) Oo, my poor back!

MRS. F.

It was your feet this afternoon.

SYLVIA (*snappily*)

Well, it's me back now, so there.

ETHEL (*gathering up the parcel*)

I'll take this into the kitchen.

SYLVIA

This house smells a bit damp, if you ask me.

ETHEL (*as she goes out*)

All houses smell damp when you first move into 'em.

SYLVIA (*sinking down on to a packing case*)

Oh dear, I thought I was going to have one of my attacks just as I turned into Abbeville Road. I 'ad to lean against a pillar box.

MRS. F.

I suppose you didn't think to remember my peppermints?

SYLVIA

Yes, I did. They're in my bag. (*She fumbles in her bag.*) Here. . . .

MRS. F. (*taking them*)

Well, thank 'eaven for small mercies—want one?

SYLVIA

No, thanks, I daren't. What's that hammering?

MRS. F.

Frank. 'E's putting up the curtains in the front bedroom.

SYLVIA

I shall be glad when we're settled in and no mistake. What a day!

ETHEL (*returning*)

There's no opener!

MRS. F.

Frank's got one on his penknife.

ETHEL (*going into the hall and shouting*)

Frank—Frank.

FRANK (*upstairs*)

What's up?

ETHEL

Chuck us down your penknife, we want the opener for the baked beans.

FRANK

'Arf a mo' . . . Here you are . . . Coming down.
(*There is a moment's pause, and then the penknife falls at* ETHEL's *feet. She comes back into the room.*)

ETHEL

Here, Syl, go and fix 'em, there's a dear. I've got to get this room straight. Mother, you might go and help her. I've laid

21

half the table and the saucepans are on the floor by the dresser.

SYLVIA (*taking opener*)
No peace for the wicked.

ETHEL
Go on, Mother, you've sat there quite long enough.

MRS. F.
We ought to have kept Gladys an extra day and made her 'elp us with the move. . . .

ETHEL
Gladys was more trouble than she was worth. I'd rather do for myself.

MRS. F.
All very fine for you. You're a young woman—wait till you get to my age. . . . (*She gets up resentfully.*)

ETHEL
Go on, Mother—I'll be in in a minute. I put the butter on the window sill.
(SYLVIA *and* MRS. FLINT *go out.* ETHEL, *left alone, continues straightening the room. She hums a little song to herself as she does so. After a few moments* FRANK *comes in. He is an ordinary-looking man of thirty-five. He carries a hammer and a bag of tintacks. These he puts down on the sideboard.*)

FRANK
I just tacked 'em up for the time being. We'll 'ave to take 'em down again when the blinds come.

ETHEL

Supper'll be ready soon.

FRANK

You look tired. You've been doing too much.

ETHEL

Don't talk so silly.

FRANK

You've been at it all day, you know.

ETHEL

What do you expect me to do—sit down by the fire and read a nice book?

FRANK

All right, snappy!
(*He puts his arm round her shoulder and they stand looking out into the garden.*)
They haven't 'arf left that garden in a mess. Wait till I get after it. Bit of luck about that May tree, isn't it?

ETHEL

I never noticed it.

FRANK

You wouldn't.

ETHEL

Fat lot of time I've had to stand around looking at May trees.

FRANK

Where's Percy?

23

ETHEL

He started miaouing his 'ead off the moment we got here, so I let him out. He's up to no good, I shouldn't wonder.

FRANK

We ought to have 'ad him arranged when he was little.

ETHEL

Oh, Frank . . . (*She leans against him.*) D'you like it?

FRANK

Like what?

ETHEL

The house, silly, you haven't said a word.

FRANK

Of course I like it.

ETHEL

I can't hardly believe it, you know, not really, it's all been so quick. You being demobbed and coming home and getting the job through Mr. Baxter and now here we are moved in all inside of six weeks!

FRANK

Good old Baxter. We ought to drink his health.

ETHEL

We 'aven't got anything to drink it in except Sylvia's Wincarnis.

FRANK

Well, 'e'll 'ave to take the will for the deed.

ETHEL (*suddenly sitting down*)
Oh dear!

FRANK

What's up?

ETHEL

I don't know—I just can't get over not having that awful weight on me mind all the time.

FRANK

How d'you mean?

ETHEL

Oh, you know.

FRANK

Me perishing on a field of slaughter? What a chance!

ETHEL

There was a chance every minute of every day for four years and don't you forget it. I used to feel sick every time the postman came, every time the bell rang.

FRANK

Well, there's no sense in going on about it now, it's all over and done with.

ETHEL

We're lucky; it isn't so over and done with for some people. Look at poor old Mrs. Worsley, two sons gone and her husband, nothing left to live for, and Mrs. Cross with that boy she was so proud of done in for life, can't even feed himself properly. We're lucky all right; we ought to be grateful. . . .

FRANK

Who to?

ETHEL

Now then, Frank . . .

25

FRANK

All right, I won't start any arguments—you can say your prayers till kingdom come if you like, but you can't expect me to, not after all I've seen. I don't 'old with a God who just singles a few out to be nice to, and lets all the others rot. 'E can get on with it for all I care.

ETHEL

It's wrong to talk like that, Frank, it's blasphemous.

FRANK

Sorry, old girl. I've got to talk the way I feel.

ETHEL

Well, I think you ought to feel different from what you do.

FRANK

That's as may be, but you can't 'elp your feelings, can you? I'm back, aren't I? That's a fact. Instead of lying out there dead in a shell 'ole I'm standing 'ere alive. In Number 17 Sycamore Road, Clapham Common. That's another fact. It's nobody's fault, not mine or yours or God's or anyone's; it just 'appened like that.

ETHEL

You went to the war because it was your duty and it s no use you pretending you didn't.

FRANK

I went to the war because I wanted to.

ETHEL

Would you go again?

FRANK

I expect so.

26

ETHEL (*almost crying*)

I wouldn't let you, see? Not again! I'd rather kill you with my own hands.

FRANK

That'd be just plain silly.

ETHEL

You give me a headache talking like that; it doesn't make sense.

FRANK

What does make sense, I'd like to know?

ETHEL (*heatedly*)

Lots of things. There's me and the children, isn't there? There's your job, there's this house and the life we've got to live in it, and you spoil everything by talking about war and saying you'd go again if anyone asked you to. . . .

FRANK

I never said that at all.

ETHEL

Oh yes, you did, you know you did, and I just can't bear to think of it—not after all I've been through, waiting for you and wondering about you—it's cruel to make me even think of it.

FRANK

What's the use of upsetting yourself? There isn't going to be another war, anyway.

ETHEL

There'll always be wars as long as men are such fools as to want to go to them.

27

FRANK (*gently, sitting down next to her*)
Well, let's stop talking about it now, shall we? Everything's all right. You're here, I'm here, the children are fine, except for Queenie's tonsils, and we've got a home of our own at last. Everything's more than all right, it's wonderful.

ETHEL (*burying her head on his shoulder*)
Oh, Frank . . .

FRANK
Poor old girl—living four years with your mother can't 'ave been all jam, I will say. I think I was better off in the trenches.

ETHEL (*muffled*)
You ought to be ashamed, saying such things.

FRANK
Oh, your mother's all right in her way, but that house in Battersea, oh dear! It gave me the willies after five weeks, let alone four years. At least we've got a bath now that doesn't scratch the hide off of you.

ETHEL
Lend me your 'anky.

FRANK (*giving her his handkerchief*)
Here you are.

ETHEL (*blowing her nose*)
I must go and 'elp Mother and Syl with the supper.

FRANK (*turning her round*)
'Ere, let's have a look at you.

ETHEL
What for?

28

FRANK

Just to see what's 'appened to your face. I don't seem to 'ave 'ad time for a really good look since I've been back.

ETHEL

Stop it . . . Leave off . . .

FRANK

'Old still a minute.

ETHEL

Now see here, Frank Gibbons . . . (*She wriggles but without conviction.*)

FRANK

Well, it's not a bad face as faces go, I will say. . . .

ETHEL

Thanks very much, I'm sure.

FRANK

And of course it's not quite as young as it was when I married it.

ETHEL

Leave 'old of me!

FRANK

But still, taken by and large, I wouldn't change it! I might wipe some of the dirt off the side of it, but I wouldn't change it!

ETHEL (*struggling to get up*)
Dirt—where?

FRANK (*firmly*)
Keep still—'ere—— (*He rubs the side of her face with his handkerchief.*) That's better—now then——

29

ETHEL

Now then what?

FRANK

Give us a kiss.

ETHEL

I'll do no such thing.

FRANK

Why not, may I ask?

ETHEL

Because we haven't got no time for fooling about, and well
you know it. . . .

FRANK

Oh—turning nasty, are we? We'll soon see about that.

ETHEL

Frank Gibbons——

FRANK (*kissing her firmly*)

Shut up.

(*At this moment* BOB MITCHELL *appears at the french
window and taps politely. He is a pleasant-looking man
of thirty-seven.* ETHEL *and* FRANK *jump up.*)

BOB

I hope I don't intrude?

ETHEL

Oh dear!

BOB

I live at number fifteen next door, and my missus and I
thought if you needed anything in the way of groceries or
what-not . . .

30

FRANK (*staring at him*)
Well, I'll be damned!

ETHEL
Frank!

FRANK
Mitchell—Bob Mitchell!

BOB (*a little puzzled*)
That's right.

FRANK
Don't you remember me—Frank Gibbons, the Buffs, B Company, Festubert 1915?

BOB
My God! It's old Gibbo!
(*They rush at each other, shake hands and slap each other on the back.*)

ETHEL
Well, I never . . .

FRANK
You old son of a gun!

BOB
My God, I thought you was dead as mutton after that night attack—when we'd gone on to Givenchy and left your lot in the mud. . . .

FRANK
Me dead as mutton! I'm tougher than that—only one small 'ole through me leg in four years. . . . How did you make out?

31

BOB

Not so bad—got gassed in 1917, but I'm all right now—made me chest a bit weak, that's all.

FRANK

Well, I'll say it's a small world and no mistake.

ETHEL

Don't you think you'd better introduce me, Frank?

FRANK

Of course—this is my wife, Bob.

BOB

Pleased to meet you, Mrs. Gibbons.

ETHEL

It's a pleasure, I'm sure.

BOB

What a coincidence—I can't get over it.

FRANK

How long have you been here?

BOB

Over a year now—we took the house when I got me discharge in March 1918. I couldn't do any work for a while, but I had me pension and Nora—that's my missus—had a little put by, but now I'm doing fine—in the insurance business. (*To* ETHEL.) Nora would have come herself, but she's a bit under the weather tonight. You see, we're expecting a little stranger almost any day now, and——

ETHEL

It's not her first, is it?

BOB

Oh no—we've got a boy of fourteen—he wants to be a sailor —and we had a girl, too, but she died in 1916 just after I'd gone back after me first leave. . . .

FRANK

What a coincidence! What a coincidence! After four bloody years.

ETHEL

Frank!

FRANK

Well, if they weren't bloody, nothing was!

ETHEL

I'm afraid we haven't anything to offer you, Mr. Mitchell— you see, everything's upside down. . . .

FRANK

He can stay and have whatever we're 'aving.

BOB

No, thanks, all the same—I'll have to be getting back to Nora.

FRANK

We've got to celebrate this somehow.

BOB

I've got a bottle of Johnnie Walker next door—it won't take a minute.

ETHEL

You two stay here—I'll go and fetch Sylvia's Wincarnis. (*She runs out.*)

FRANK

Oh dear!

BOB

It won't take me a minute to get the whisky.

FRANK

Here, whose dugout d'you think this is? I'll pop in and 'ave one with you later.

BOB

Have you got a job yet?

FRANK

Yes—I had a bit of luck—a chap called Baxter in my regiment, he was drafted out to Arras in February and before the war he was running a sort of travel agency in Oxford Street—well, he got a Blighty one and was invalided 'ome, and believe it or not, 'e was the first one I run into when I got back last April. He'd started his business again, and things were beginning to pick up so he gave me a job.

BOB

Travel agency—whew!

FRANK

Tours of the battlefields, I'll thank you.

BOB (*laughing*)

That's a good one.

FRANK

Some people certainly do have queer ways of enjoying themselves.

BOB

You've got kids, haven't you? I remember you talking about them.

FRANK

Yes, three. Two girls and a boy. They're with Ethel's aunt in Broadstairs. We didn't want them under our feet while we were moving in.

BOB

How old are they?

FRANK

Reg, that's the boy, 'e's twelve; Queenie's thirteen, and Vi's fourteen.

BOB

My Billy's getting on for fifteen.

FRANK

Seems funny, this, doesn't it? When you think of the last time we 'ad a jaw—remember that canteen?

BOB

Just before Christmas, wasn't it? The night before you went up to the line. What was her name, that Lady Something-or-other behind the bar, the one that called you her poor dear?

FRANK

What was it? I can see her now—a fair knockout she was.

BOB

What happened to old Shorty?

FRANK

You mean the little fat chap with red hair in my company?

35

BOB

That's him.

FRANK

'E got 'is on the Somme, poor bastard, 'adn't been out of the trench two seconds when, wallop, out 'e went!

BOB

Nice and quick and no hurt feelings.

FRANK

You've said it.

> (ETHEL *returns with a bottle of Wincarnis and two glasses.*)

ETHEL

Here you are—supper will be ready in a minute. Are you sure you won't stay and take pot luck with us, Mr. Mitchell?

BOB

Thanks very much, Mrs. Gibbons, but I really must get back.

ETHEL

Will you ask your wife when it would be convenient for me to pop in and see her?

BOB

Any time—any time at all.

ETHEL

Well, I'll be saying good night, Mr. Mitchell.

FRANK

Aren't you going to have a drop?

ETHEL

No, dear, it would spoil my supper. Don't be long.

BOB

Don't forget—if there's anything you're wanting——

ETHEL

Thank you very much, I'm sure. Good night.

BOB

Good night.
> (ETHEL *goes out.* FRANK *pours out the Wincarnis.*)

FRANK (*handing a glass to* BOB)
Here you are, old man.

BOB

Thanks.

FRANK

It tastes a bit funny, but it's better than nothing.

BOB

Happy days!

FRANK

Happy days!
> (THEY *drink as*

THE LIGHTS FADE.)

SCENE II

December, 1925.

SCENE
It is about three o'clock on Christmas afternoon. Christmas dinner is over. VI, QUEENIE, REG, SAM LEADBITTER, *and* PHYLLIS BLAKE *are still sitting at the table wearing paper hats, having port and nuts and pulling crackers. The chairs of* FRANK, ETHEL, SYLVIA, *and* MRS. FLINT *are empty as they have retired to the rarely used front room in order to leave the young people alone.* VI *is a pleasant, nondescript-looking girl of twenty;* QUEENIE, *who is a year younger, is prettier and a trifle flashy.* REG, *aged eighteen, is a nice-looking, intelligent boy.* SAM LEADBITTER, *who is about a year older than* REG, *is rather farouche in appearance. He is intense, without much humour, and slightly aware of intellectual superiority.* REG *admires him extravagantly.* PHYLLIS BLAKE, *who is a friend of* QUEENIE'S, *is a gentle, matter-of-fact girl of about eighteen. As the curtain rises,* REG *is starting to make a speech.*

REG
I will now propose a toast to the two strangers within our gates. . . .

QUEENIE
'Ark at him!

VI
Shut up, Queenie.

REG (*ignoring the interruption*)
Welcome, thrice welcome, Sam Leadbitter and Phyllis Blake. (*He raises his glass of port and makes a signal for everyone to drink.*)

QUEENIE
You ought to have mentioned the lady first.

REG (*grandly*)
Sweeping aside the annoying interruptions of my young sister, who is being far too bossy, as usual, I will now call upon my old and valued friend, Sam Leadbitter, to say a few words.

QUEENIE
Old and valued friend! You've only known 'im since August Bank Holiday—chuck us the nut crackers, Phyl——

VI
Speech! Speech! Speech! Oh dear! (*She giggles.*)

REG
Come on, Sam.

QUEENIE
Get it off your chest, Sam, Edie'll be in to clear in a minute. (*Amid loud applause* SAM *rises to his feet.*)

SAM
Ladies and gentlemen—comrades——

QUEENIE

Make up your mind.

REG

You're asking for it, you know, Queenie, and if you don't shut up being saucy, you'll get it! Go on, Sam, don't take no notice of her.

SAM

Comrades—in thanking you for your kind hospitality on this festive day, I would like to say that it is both a pleasure and a privilege to be here. . . .

QUEENIE

Hear—hear——

SAM

Though as you know, holding the views I do, it's really against my principles to hobnob to any great extent with the bourgeoisie. . . .

QUEENIE

What's that?

VI

I think it means common in a nice way.

REG

Order!

SAM

I cannot help but feel that today, what with being Christmas and one thing and another, it would be but right and proper to put aside all prejudice and class hatred. . . .

QUEENIE

Very nice of you, I'm sure.

SAM

As you well know, there are millions and millions of homes in this country today where Christmas is naught but a mockery, where there is neither warmth nor food nor even the bare necessities of life, where little children, old before their time, huddle round a fireless grate. . . .

QUEENIE

They'd be just as well off if they stayed in the middle of the room then, wouldn't they?

REG

Shut up, Queenie, Sam's quite right.

SAM (*sternly*)

That sort of remark, Queenie, springs from complacency, arrogance and a full stomach!

QUEENIE

You leave my stomach out of it!

SAM (*warming up*)

It is people like you, apathetic, unthinking, docile supporters of a capitalistic system which is a disgrace to civilisation, who are responsible for at least three quarters of the cruel suffering of the world! You never trouble to look below the surface of things, do you? And for why? Because you and your whole class are servers of Mammon! Money's all you think about. As long as you can earn your miserable little salaries and go to the pictures and enjoy yourselves and have a roof over your head and a bed to sleep in and food to eat, the rest of suffering humanity can go hang, can't it? You'll accept any conditions, no matter how degrading, as long as *you're* all right, as long as your petty security isn't interfered with. It doesn't matter to you that the greatest struggle for the betterment of mankind that has ever been in the history of the world is going on under your noses! Oh dear no, you haven't even noticed it; you're too busy getting all weepy about Rudolph Valentino to spare any tears for the workers of the world whose whole lives are made hideous by oppression, injustice, and capitalistic greed!

VI

Don't get excited, Sam, Queenie didn't mean it.

SAM (*violently*)

I am not excited. Queenie doesn't mean anything to me, anyway.

QUEENIE

Pardon me all, while I go and commit suicide!

SAM

But what she represents, what she symbolises, means a great deal. She is only one of the millions who, when the great day comes, will be swept out of existence like so much chaff on the wind. . . .

QUEENIE

Well, it's nice to know, isn't it?

SAM (*sitting down abruptly*)

I've said my say, thank you very much.

REG (*dutifully*)

Hear, hear—bravo!

QUEENIE

I don't know what you're saying bravo about, I'm sure. I think Sam's been very rude.

43

REG

You don't understand, Queenie; if you did, you wouldn't
have kept interrupting all the time and trying to be funny.
Sam's quite right in everything he says, only you just haven't
got enough sense to see it.

QUEENIE

I suppose you understand all of it, don't you?

REG

No, I don't, but I'm trying to.

QUEENIE

I suppose we shall soon be having you standing up on a
soap box in Hyde Park and making a fathead of yourself!

VI

Run and tell Edie we're ready for her to clear now, Queenie,
say we'll help her—the boys can go into the front room;
we've left Mum and Dad and Granny alone quite long
enough.

REG (*with sarcasm*)

Maybe if we asked her nicely, Aunt Sylvia'd sing us the
Indian Love Lyrics!

VI

And don't talk in that tone about poor Aunt Sylvia, she's not
feeling well.

QUEENIE (*going out of the room*)

She never is.

REG (*rising*)

Come on, Sam. Come up to my room for a minute and have
a cigarette.

VI

Better not let your father catch you.

SAM (*rising*)

I'm sorry if I was rude, Vi.

VI (*beginning to pile up the plates*)

It doesn't matter, Sam, only you can't expect everybody in the world to feel just the same as you do, you know.

REG (*hotly*)

Sam's got more knowledge and intelligence than all of us put together.

VI

If that's the case, it wouldn't do him any harm to remember it once in a while and not shout so much.

REG (*irritably*)

Come on, Sam. (*He slams out of the room, followed rather sheepishly by* SAM.)

PHYLLIS

Can I help, Vi?

VI

Yes, Phyl, you might put the preserved fruits in the sideboard cupboard, the sweets can go in there too, but leave one dish out to take into the front room.

PHYLLIS (*complying*)

Sam got quite upset, didn't he?

VI

He's a bit Bolshie, that's all that's the matter with him.

45

PHYLLIS

I didn't understand half of what he was talking about.

VI

I don't expect he understood much of it himself.

PHYLLIS

Reg thinks he's wonderful.

VI

Reg thinks anybody who can use a few long words is wonderful. He'll soon get over it.

(QUEENIE *re-enters, followed by* EDIE, *with a tray.* EDIE *is rather an unkempt girl of about twenty-five. During the following scene she and the girls manage to clear the table, change the tablecloths, and generally tidy up the room.*)

QUEENIE

Has Trotsky gone upstairs?

VI

You were awful, Queenie; if you hadn't of gone on at him the way you did, he wouldn't have got so excited.

QUEENIE (*busying herself*)

Silly great fool.

VI

You needn't stay and wash up, Edie, you can slip along home. We can do it later.

EDIE

Thanks very much.

46

VI

How's your father's neck?

EDIE

Mother was up all night poulticing it, but it was still pain-ing him terrible when I left this morning.

PHYLLIS

They say if you have one you generally have seven.

EDIE

Well, this is 'is third, so we only got four more to go.

VI (*piling things onto the tray*)

There's some crackers left in the box in the sideboard—you might care to take them home to your little brother.

EDIE (*finding them*)

Thanks ever so.

QUEENIE

Here—you can balance them on the top—that's right.
(QUEENIE *balances the box of crackers on the top of the loaded tray and* EDIE *staggers out of the room with it.* VI *and* PHYLLIS *fold up the tablecloth between them while* QUEENIE *gets the day cloth out of the sideboard drawer.*)

PHYLLIS (*to* VI)

It has been nice you letting me come and spend my Christ-mas Day with you. I don't know what I'd have done all by myself in that house in Wandsworth with Auntie ill and everything.

VI

Is she any better?

47

PHYLLIS

No, she just goes on about the same. Mrs. Watts is looking after her until seven, so I don't have to get back till about then.

QUEENIE (*helping* VI *to put on the day tablecloth*)
One of our girls at the shop's mother has been bedridden for five years—can't even get up to wash herself. Just think of that.

PHYLLIS

What some people go through!
(*There is the sound of a tap at the window.*)

QUEENIE

Good heavens, what's that? (*Going to the window.*) Only Mr. Mitchell come to talk to Dad, I expect.
(*She pulls back the curtain and opens the window. It is still more or less daylight, but there is a fog, so the outlook is rather gloomy.* BILLY MITCHELL *steps into the room. He is a nice-looking boy of about twenty-one. He is in sailor's rig only without his cap.*)
Billy, what a surprise! I thought you was going back this morning.

BILLY

No, not till tonight. Hallo—Queen——

QUEENIE

Hallo.

BILLY

Better leave the window on the latch, Dad'll be in in a minute.

48

VI (*introducing*)
Do you know Miss Blake . . . Mr. Mitchell.

BILLY (*shaking hands*)
Pleased to meet you.

QUEENIE
Have a choc?

BILLY
No, thanks, I've been eating my head off. Where's Reg?

VI
Upstairs with Sam.

BILLY
Oh, he's here, is he?

QUEENIE
I'll say he is. I wonder you didn't hear him. He's been bellowing like a bull.

BILLY
Down with the dirty capitalists?

QUEENIE
That's right.

BILLY
I know all that stuff by heart—we got a couple of 'em in my ship, not bad chaps really, you know, just got everything a bit cockeyed, that's all.

PHYLLIS
It must be lovely being a sailor.

49

BILLY

Well, I wouldn't go so far as to say lovely, exactly, but it's not bad, and you do get about. Join the Navy and see the world, you know.

QUEENIE

Go on—you've never been further than Southsea!

BILLY (*cheerfully*)

Lots of time. Next year I'll probably be sent to the China station—think of that!

QUEENIE

Well, drop us a p.c. saying you've arrived safely.

PHYLLIS

China station sounds funny, doesn't it? Like as though it was on the Underground! (*She giggles.*)

VI

We ought to go into the drawing-room now. Mum'll be wondering what's happened to us.

BILLY

Be a sport and go on in then, Vi, I want to talk to Queenie a minute.

VI

Oh, so that's how it is, is it?

QUEENIE

I don't know what you're talking about, I'm sure.

VI

Come on, Phyl, we know when we're not wanted.

QUEENIE

I don't see why we don't all go.

BILLY

I want to talk to you a minute. I just said so, didn't I?

QUEENIE

Maybe I don't want to talk to you!

BILLY

Well, if you're going to be high and mighty about it, it's all right with me. I only thought that as I was going back to duty tonight that——

VI

Of course Queenie'll stay for a minute, Billy; she's only putting on airs.

QUEENIE

You mind your own business, Vi Gibbons. I'll talk to who I like when I like.

VI

Well, nobody's stopping you—come on, Phyl. . . . See you later, Billy. Don't go without saying good-bye to Mum and Dad.

BILLY

You bet I won't.

(VI *and* PHYLLIS *go out, shutting the door after them.* QUEENIE *flounces over to the fire and sits down.*)

QUEENIE

Well?

BILLY (*grinning*)

Well, what?

51

QUEENIE

What is it you're so keen to talk to me about?

BILLY

I don't rightly know now; you being so upsiedupsie's put it right out of my head.

QUEENIE

I beg your pardon, I'm sure.

BILLY

Don't mention it—all in the day's work.

QUEENIE

Fancy asking Vi and Phyl to go out and leave us alone. You ought to have known better. I shall never hear the last of it.

BILLY

Oh, so that's what's worrying you, is it?

QUEENIE (*shrugging her shoulders*)

It's not worrying me at all. I just thought it sounded sort of silly, that's all.

BILLY

I don't see what's silly about it. Vi knows we went to the Majestic on Friday night, and she saw us with her own eyes walking down Elm Park Road on Sunday—she must guess there's something doing.

QUEENIE

Well, if she does she's wrong, so there. There isn't.

BILLY

'Ere, 'arf a minute—what's got into you, anyway? I haven't done anything wrong, have I?

52

QUEENIE

I don't like being taken for granted; no girl does.

BILLY

How d'you mean, taken for granted? You can't hold hands with someone all through *Desert Love* and the next minute expect them to treat you like the Empress of Russia!

QUEENIE

Oh, don't talk so silly.

BILLY

It's you that's silly.

QUEENIE (*getting up*)

I think we'd better go into the drawing-room.

BILLY (*turning away*)

All right, if that's the way you feel.

QUEENIE

Well, we're not doing much good here, are we? Just nagging at each other.

BILLY

Who started it?

QUEENIE

Oh—come on.

BILLY (*downcast*)

Aren't you going to kiss me good-bye? We shan't be able to in there.

QUEENIE

I should think not, indeed.

53

BILLY

Look here, Queenie, if you think I oughtn't to have said that about wanting to talk to you alone in front of Vi, I'm sorry, see? I can't say more than that, now can I?

QUEENIE (*looking down*)

No, I suppose not.

BILLY

Well, then!

QUEENIE (*with an imperceptible movement towards him*)

Oh, all right. . . .
(*He takes her in his arms and kisses her.*)

BILLY (*gently*)

I do love you, Queenie—you know that, don't you?

QUEENIE (*resting her head on his shoulder*)

Yes.

BILLY

And I wouldn't do anything to upset you—that is, not meaning to—you know that too, don't you?

QUEENIE

Oh, Billy—I wish you weren't going back so soon.

BILLY

Will you write to me every now and again? Even if it's only a postcard?

QUEENIE

If you'll write to me.

BILLY

That's easy. Promise?

54

QUEENIE

Yes—cross my heart.

BILLY

You're the sweetest girl I ever met in all my life or ever will meet, either.

QUEENIE

That's easy to say, but how do you know?

BILLY

Never you mind, it's true. I've been thinking about you all the time, ever since that sick leave I had at Whitsun, when we went to Richmond Park—do you remember?

QUEENIE

Of course I do.

BILLY

A little later on, when I'm earning a bit more, do you think we might have a shot at getting married?

QUEENIE (*turning away*)

Oh, Bill, how do I know? You might be in China or anywhere—you might have forgotten all about me by then.

BILLY

More likely to be the other way round. A pretty kid like you, working at being a manicurist, talking to all sorts of different fellows all day long . . .

QUEENIE

It isn't all jam being a sailor's wife, is it?

BILLY

It wouldn't be so bad, if I get me promotion all right and get on—don't say anything now, just think it over. . . .

QUEENIE (*with a rush*)

Oh, Billy, I wouldn't be the right sort of wife for you, really I wouldn't. I want too much—I'm always thinking about the kind of things I want and they wouldn't be the kind of things you'd want me to want.

BILLY

How do you mean?

QUEENIE

Oh, I know it sounds silly, but I'm not like Vi; she's a quiet one. I'm different. Mum sometimes says that all I think of is having a good time, but it isn't only that. . . .

BILLY

I don't see no harm in wanting to have a good time—that's what everybody wants in one way or another.

QUEENIE

I'll tell you something awful. I hate living here; I hate living in a house that's exactly like hundreds of other houses. I hate coming home from work in the Tube. I hate washing up and helping Mum darn Dad's socks and listening to Aunt Sylvia keeping on about how ill she is all the time, and what's more, I know why I hate it too; it's because it's all so common! There! I expect you'll think I'm getting above myself, and I wouldn't blame you—maybe I am, but I can't help it—that's why I don't think I'd be a good wife for you, however much I loved you—and I do. . . . I really do. . . . Oh, Billy . . . (*She bursts into tears.*)

BILLY (*putting his arms round her*)

Here, hold on, dear, there isn't anything to cry about. I know what you mean all right; it's only natural that you should feel that way about things.

QUEENIE

You don't think I'm awful then, do you? And mean?

BILLY

Of course I don't. Come on now, cheer up, you don't want to have red eyes on Christmas Day, do you?

QUEENIE (*dabbing her eyes with her handkerchief*)
I'm sorry, Bill, please forgive me. . . .
(*She suddenly kisses him and runs out of the room. He stands looking after her in perplexity for a moment, and then with a sigh goes up towards the window. He has nearly reached it when* FRANK *comes in. He hasn't really changed very much in the last six years. His figure is perhaps a shade thicker and his hair a shade greyer and thinner. At the moment he is still wearing the paper hat he got out of a cracker.*)

FRANK

Billy! What are you doing in here all by yourself?

BILLY

I've been talking to Queenie.

FRANK

Was that her rushing upstairs just now?

BILLY

Yes—I think it was.

FRANK (*quizzically*)
Oh, I see.

BILLY

I just popped in to say good-bye——

57

FRANK

A bit miserable having to go back to work on Christmas night, isn't it?

BILLY

Oh, I dunno—it's all right once you're there.

FRANK

How old are you now, Billy?

BILLY

Getting on for twenty-one.

FRANK

Wish I was.

BILLY (*with an effort*)

Mr. Gibbons——

FRANK

Yes, son?

BILLY

If in two or three years' time, when I've worked my way up a bit, Queenie and me got married, would you mind?

FRANK

If Queenie wanted to, it wouldn't matter whether I minded or not. She'd get her own way; she always does.

BILLY (*ruefully*)

She's certainly got a will of her own all right.

FRANK

Anyway, a lot can happen between now and three years.

58

BILLY

You see, I leave the ship I'm in now round about April, and next commission I'll probably be drafted for foreign service. By the time I get back, I ought to be drawing higher pay if I've been behaving myself.

FRANK

What does Queenie think about it?

BILLY

That's the trouble—I think she thinks that being a sailor's wife might be rather hard going. . . .

FRANK

She likes having a good time, our Queenie, but maybe she'll calm down later on. Here's hoping, anyhow.

BILLY

If you get a chance, Mr. Gibbons, you might put in a good word for me every now and again.

FRANK (*smiling*)

Righto, son, I'll do my best.

BILLY

Thanks, Mr. Gibbons. I think I'll be getting along now. Mother always gets a bit depressed on my last day of leave.

FRANK

How is she?

BILLY

As well as can be expected.

FRANK

Aren't you going into the front room?

59

BILLY

I'd rather not, if you don't mind.

FRANK

All right—I'll say good-bye for you.

BILLY

Thank you again, Mr. Gibbons.

FRANK

Go on, 'op it—good luck!

(*They shake hands solemnly.* BILLY *goes out through the french window.* FRANK, *left alone, takes a Gold Flake out of a packet in his pocket, lights it, and balances it on the edge of the mantelpiece while he puts some more coal on the fire. Then he settles himself comfortably in an armchair. From the drawing-room comes the sound of the piano and* SYLVIA's *voice singing "When I Am Dying." The door opens gently, and* ETHEL *slips into the room.*)

ETHEL

Frank, you are awful creeping out like that. You knew Sylvia was going to sing.

FRANK

What about you?

ETHEL

I came to find you.

FRANK

Oh yes, we know all about that.

ETHEL

D'you want the light on?

FRANK
No, it's all right like this—come and sit down.

ETHEL (*sitting near him*)
Edie's gone home; the girls are going to do the washing up after tea.

FRANK
Is Reg in there?

ETHEL
Yes, he came in a minute ago with that Sam Leadbitter.

FRANK (*chuckling*)
What's the betting they've been smoking themselves silly up in Reg's room?

ETHEL
Well, it is Christmas. I don't think much of that Sam Leadbitter taken all round; he seems a bit soft to me.

FRANK
I wouldn't call him soft exactly.

ETHEL
Well, you know what I mean—all that talking big—he'll get himself into trouble one of these days, you mark my words.

FRANK
He'll grow out of it. I used to shoot me neck off to beat the band when I was his age.

ETHEL
Not like he does, though, all that stuff about world revolution and the great day and down with everything—you had more sense than that. Anyhow, I wouldn't mind so much if

61

it wasn't for Reg taking every word he says as gospel—we'll be having him with long hair and a red tie soon if we're not careful.

FRANK

I shouldn't say a word if I was you; let 'em get it out of their systems.

ETHEL

It is wrong, isn't it? All that Bolshie business?

FRANK

Oh, there's something to be said for it; there's always something to be said for everything. Where they go wrong is trying to get things done too quickly. We don't like doing things quickly in this country. It's like gardening; someone once said we was a nation of gardeners, and they weren't far out. We're used to planting things and watching them grow and looking out for changes in the weather. . . .

ETHEL

You and your gardening!

FRANK

Well, it's true—think what a mess there'd be if all the flowers and vegetables and crops came popping up all in a minute. That's what all these social reformers are trying to do, trying to alter the way of things all at once. We've got our own way of settling things; it may be slow and it may be a bit dull, but it suits us all right and it always will.

ETHEL

Oh, do listen to Sylvia, she's off on "Bird of Love Divine" now, and you know how it always makes Reg laugh!

FRANK
Poor old Sylvia!

ETHEL
We ought to go back, really; it'll be tea-time in a minute.

FRANK
It's cosy in here.

ETHEL (*settling herself against him*)
Getting quite dark, isn't it?

(*They sit together in silence as*

THE LIGHTS FADE.)

SCENE III

TIME

May, 1926.

SCENE

It is late in the evening, about ten-thirty. The french windows are open as it is very warm. MRS. FLINT *is sitting in an armchair by the fireplace.* ETHEL, SYLVIA, VI, *and* QUEENIE *are at the table having supper, which consists of cold ham, tomatoes, cheese, pickles, and tea.*

ETHEL

Run into the kitchen, Queenie, there's a dear, and see if the soup's all right. Dad ought to be home soon; it's getting on for eleven.

QUEENIE (*rising reluctantly*)

All right, if my legs will get me that far.

ETHEL

When you've done that you'd better go to bed—you, too, Vi, you must be dog tired, all that standing about . . .

QUEENIE (*as she goes*)

I wonder if they'll open up the shop again tomorrow—I'll have to go along in the morning and see.

65

VI

Are you going to wait up for Dad, Mum?

ETHEL

Yes, I'm all right—they said in Regent's Park his shift would be back before ten. I wish I hadn't missed him with those sandwiches. Seems silly trailing all that way for nothing. . . .

SYLVIA

Feels sort of flat now, doesn't it? It all being over, I mean.

MRS. F.

It's wicked, that's what it is, downright wicked, those strikers upsetting the whole country like that. . . .

ETHEL

I wish Reg'd come home; I wish I knew where he was.

VI

I'll give that Sam Leadbitter a piece of my mind when I see him. Encouraging Reg to make a fool of himself . . . I'll tell him off, you see if I don't.

ETHEL

Telling people off's no good when they think they're in the right.

SYLVIA

I was talking to Mr. Rogers only a couple of weeks ago—his brother works up North, you know—and he said that conditions were something terrible, he did really.

ETHEL

I'm so afraid something's happened to him.

66

VI
Don't worry, Mother; worrying never does any good any-how.

ETHEL
I can't help it.

SYLVIA
Mr. Rogers says this is only just the beginning of a whole lot more trouble—he says the Government may have won this time, but next time it won't be so easy.

VI
A fat lot he knows about it. He never sets foot outside that shop of his from one year's end to another.

SYLVIA
Mr. Rogers is a very clever man, Vi—he's a great reader too. Why, you never see him without he's got a book in his hand.

VI
I shouldn't think he sold much at that rate.

MRS. F.
You and your Mr. Rogers.

SYLVIA
He's been very kind to me and I like him, so there.

MRS. F.
Like him! I should just think you did—we get nothing but Mr. Rogers this and Mr. Rogers that from morning till night. I'd like to know what Mrs. Rogers has to say about it, I must say.

SYLVIA

Now look here, Mrs. Flint, if you're insinuating——

MRS. F.

You give me a pain, Sylvia, really you do, the way you keep on about that man. Just because he pays you a few shillings every now and again for designing them Christmas cards and calendars, you're doing nothing more nor less than throwing yourself at his head.

SYLVIA (*furious*)

Mrs. Flint, how can you!

ETHEL (*wearily*)

Oh, do shut up, you two—I've got enough to think about without listening to you snapping at each other. Sylvia can go and live with Mr. Rogers for all I care.

SYLVIA

That's a nice way to talk, Ethel, I must say.

ETHEL

Now look here, Sylvia, I'm tired, see? We're all tired. And what's more, I'm worried to death about Reg. I 'aven't slept properly for three nights wondering what's happened to him. I know Vi had that message from Sam saying he was all right, but I shan't believe he is until I see him. If on top of all that I have to hear you and Mother go on nag, nag, nag at each other over nothing at all, I shall lose my temper, and that's a fact. You never stop, either of you, and I'm sick to death of it.

MRS. F.

I'm sure I haven't said anything.

ETHEL

Oh yes, you have. You're always giving Sylvia sly digs about Mr. Rogers. You know perfectly well Sylvia isn't strong enough to do any steady work, and the odd commissions she gets from that novelty shop come in very handy. If Mr. Rogers has taken a fancy to her, so much the better; she's old enough to look after herself, 'eaven knows, and if he murdered his wife and strangled his children and run off to Australia with her, it still wouldn't be anything to do with you, so shut up!

MRS. F. (*struggling to get out of her chair*)

Help me up—help me up—I'm not going to stay here and be insulted by my own daughter.

ETHEL

You're not being insulted by anyone, be quiet.

SYLVIA

It's all my fault—I'm in the way in this house and I always have been and you needn't think I don't know it.

ETHEL

It's a pity you've stayed so long then.

SYLVIA (*bursting into tears*)

Oh, Ethel, how can you! I'll leave tomorrow; I'll never set foot in the house again. . . .

MRS. F.

And a good job too.

VI

Oh, don't cry, Auntie Sylvia. Mother didn't mean it. She's nervy tonight; we all are. . . .

69

SYLVIA (*sobbing*)

I don't care how nervy she is; if only I had my health and strength I'm sure I wouldn't have to be beholden to anybody.

MRS. F.

Health and strength indeed! You're as strong as a cart horse!

ETHEL

Take your grandmother up to bed, Vi, for God's sake.

VI

Come on, Granny—I'll help you upstairs.

ETHEL

Stop crying, Sylvia—I didn't mean what I said. I don't know which way to turn tonight, what with one thing and another.

MRS. F. (*shaking* VI *off*)

I can manage by myself, thank you.

SYLVIA

If you wished to hurt me, you've certainly succeeded——

ETHEL

Nobody wished to hurt you. Do stop crying, you'll only give yourself one of your headaches.

(QUEENIE *comes into the room.*)

QUEENIE

What in the world's happening? I thought the strikers had got in!

VI

It's only Auntie Sylvia and Granny, as usual.

SYLVIA

That's right, blame me! Everything's always my fault.

MRS. F.

I'm an old woman and the sooner I'm dead the better—I know you're all itching to see me in my coffin.

VI

Don't talk so silly, Granny, come on upstairs.

MRS. F.

It's coming to something when your own flesh and blood turns on you as if you was a criminal.

VI

Never mind, Gran, it'll all be forgiven and forgotten in the morning.

(VI *leads* MRS. FLINT, *still talking, from the room.* ETHEL *puts her head wearily down on her arms.* QUEENIE *goes over to her.*)

QUEENIE

Have another cup of tea, Mum, it'll buck you up.

ETHEL

I'm all right.

QUEENIE

Here—I'll pour it out.

ETHEL

You'd better give your aunt Sylvia a cup of tea.

SYLVIA (*bridling*)

I don't want anyone to put themselves out on my account, I'm sure.

71

QUEENIE (*pouring out a cup of tea*)

Nobody is, Aunt Sylvia. Here you are; the sugar's just by you. Here you are, Mum.

ETHEL

Thank you, dear. Now slip along up to bed, there's a good girl.

QUEENIE

I'd rather wait till Dad comes. He can't be long now.

ETHEL

Very well.

SYLVIA (*with martyred politeness*)

Would you like me to wait up for Frank, Ethel, and you go to bed?

ETHEL

No, thanks, Sylvia—I couldn't sleep, anyway.

SYLVIA

I've been sleeping terribly badly lately, what with all the upset and the heat and everything. . . .

ETHEL

Go on up now then and take an aspirin.

SYLVIA

I daren't, it always makes my heart go funny. Dr. Morgan says it does do that with some people. He gave me some tablets, but I'm afraid they're not much good. I'll take two tonight just to see what happens.

72

ETHEL

I shouldn't overdo it if I was you.

SYLVIA

They're quite harmless. (*She gets up.*) I'll take my tea up with me.

ETHEL (*relieved*)

Nothing like a nice cup of tea in bed.

SYLVIA (*smiling wanly*)

Good night, Ethel—good night, Queenie.

QUEENIE

Good night, Aunt Sylvia.

ETHEL

Good night, Syl, sleep well.

SYLVIA (*going out*)

I'm afraid there's not much hope of that!

ETHEL

Poor Sylvia, she's a bit of a trial sometimes.

QUEENIE

I don't know how you stand her, Mum.

ETHEL

She hasn't got anybody but us, you know. I wouldn't like to think of her living all by herself; she couldn't afford it anyhow.

QUEENIE

She could if she did a bit of work.

73

ETHEL

Well, she's tried once or twice, and it's never been any good. Remember when she answered that advertisement in 1923 and got herself to Bexhill as a companion to Mrs. Phillips? Oh dear! (*She laughs.*)

QUEENIE (*also laughing*)

She was home inside two weeks and in bed for four.

ETHEL

If it hadn't been for poor Bertie getting killed in the war, she'd have been all right, I expect.

QUEENIE

What was he like?

ETHEL

A bit soppy, I always thought, but still she liked him.

QUEENIE

How awful to be so dependent on a man living or dying that it could ruin your whole life. I don't think I ever would be.

ETHEL

Well, don't be too sure. If your dad had gone I wouldn't have been the woman I am today, far from it.

QUEENIE

You wouldn't have gone on moping about it always though, would you?

ETHEL

I don't rightly know. My heart would have broke and I suppose I should have had to put it together again as best I could.

QUEENIE
Oh, Mum!

ETHEL
What is it?

QUEENIE
You do make me feel awful sometimes.

ETHEL
Good 'eavens, child, why?

QUEENIE
Oh, you just do.

ETHEL (*looking at her out of the corner of her eye*)
Heard from Billy since he went?

QUEENIE (*offhand*)
Oh yes, just a post card with a camel on it.

ETHEL
A camel?

QUEENIE
Yes, his ship stopped somewhere where there was camels, and so he sent me a picture of one.

ETHEL
His poor mother misses him something dreadful. We all miss him really, don't we?

QUEENIE (*looking away*)
Yes—I suppose we do.
(*There is the sound of the front doorbell.*)

75

ETHEL (*sharply*)

There's the bell!

QUEENIE (*jumping up*)

I'll go!

(*She runs into the hall, but* VI *has opened the door before her. There is the sound of voices and* PHYLLIS BLAKE *comes in, followed by* VI *and* QUEENIE.)

PHYLLIS

Please forgive me for calling so late, Mrs. Gibbons, but I just popped over on my bike to see if Reg had come back yet.

VI

Well, he hasn't.

ETHEL

That's all right, dear, sit down and have a cup of tea.

PHYLLIS

Thanks very much, Mrs. Gibbons, I must be getting back in a minute.

ETHEL (*at the table*)

Time for one cup anyway. (*She pours it out.*)

QUEENIE

Dad's not back either, but he's due at any minute; him and Mr. Mitchell next door have been driving a bus.

PHYLLIS

Both of them?

VI

Mr. Mitchell's the conductor.

PHYLLIS

Have you heard from Reg, Mrs. Gibbons?

ETHEL

No, I'm afraid not, dear. He's off somewhere with Sam Lead-bitter and those men at that club they belong to—I don't know what they've been up to, I'm sure.

VI

I went to Sam's bookshop in the Tottenham Court Road two days ago, the day Reg had a row with Dad and slammed out and said he wasn't coming back, and Sam said he was all right but he'd promised not to tell where he was until the strike was over.

QUEENIE

Mother's afraid he might have got himself into trouble.

PHYLLIS

He'll be all right, Mrs. Gibbons, don't you worry.

ETHEL

I can't help it, I'm afraid. You read in those nasty bits of newspaper they hand round about there being riots and people being arrested and houses being burnt down and soldiers charging the crowds and all sorts of horrors. . . .

QUEENIE

You can't always believe what you read in the papers, even little ones.

VI

If you ask me, I shouldn't think he's been doing anything at all but run around the streets hollering; that's all any of 'em seem to do.

77

ETHEL (*hopelessly*)

I wish he'd come back, whatever he's been doing. I wish your dad hadn't gone at him like that. I shan't have a moment's peace until I know he's safe.

VI

I'm going to see that Sam Leadbitter again tomorrow morning first thing, and if he won't tell me where Reg is I'll stand in the shop and yell until he does.

(*At this moment there is a great commotion outside in the garden.* FRANK's *and* BOB's *voices are heard singing* "Rule Britannia" *at the top of their lungs. They come in, grimy but gay.*)

FRANK (*striking an attitude in front of* ETHEL)

. . . Britons never, never, never shall be slaves!

ETHEL

'Old your noise, Frank Gibbons, you'll wake up the whole street.

FRANK

Who cares! We have come unscathed, my friend and I, through untold perils, and you grumble about a bit of noise.

ETHEL

You've come unscathed through a few public houses, too, or I'm no judge.

BOB

Well, there's no denying, Mrs. G., we had a couple at the Plough with Captain Burchell, who brought us all the way from Baker Street in his car, and then just one more next door with me.

FRANK

That makes three all told, not so bad when you come to think we've saved our country from the 'orrors of bloody revolution.

ETHEL

And don't swear neither. You'd better go and wash while I dish up your supper. You'll stay and have a bite, won't you, Bob?

BOB

No, thanks all the same. Nora's got something for me next door.

FRANK

Have a drink?

ETHEL

You've had quite enough drink, Frank, and well you know it.

BOB

Better not, old man. Ethel's right, the women are always right; that's why we cherish them, isn't it? Queenie?

ETHEL

You'd better cherish yourself next door, Bob Mitchell. Nora'll be having one of her upsets if she's got something hot ready for you and you're not there to eat it.

BOB

All right, all right—I thought I'd just deliver your old man safe and sound into your loving arms. Good night, all.

FRANK

That's right, drive my best pal out of the house; that's all the thanks he gets for saving my life.

79

ETHEL

How d'you mean, saving your life?

FRANK

An old lady at Cricklewood attacked me with an umbrella, and quick as a flash he wrested it from her and hit her on the bottom with it!

VI (*giggling*)

Oh, Dad, you are awful!

FRANK

Good night, cock, see you tomorrow.

BOB

Righto, sweet dreams. Toodle-ooo, everybody! (*He goes out again, through the french windows.*)

ETHEL

Go on, Frank. (*She starts cutting some bread.*) Here, Queenie, this bread's like iron, run into the kitchen and make your dad a bit of toast while I get the soup; the toaster's on the dresser.

QUEENIE (*taking the bread and going out*)

All right, Mum.

(FRANK *goes out after her.*)

VI

I'll get the soup, Mother; you stay here, you're tired.

PHYLLIS

Can I help?

ETHEL

No, thank you, dear.

(VI *goes out.* ETHEL *sits down in the armchair by the fireplace.*)

PHYLLIS

Mr. Gibbons and Mr. Mitchell were in the war together, weren't they?

ETHEL

Yes, and to hear them talk, you'd think they were the only ones that was. (*There is the sound of the front doorbell.*) There's the bell! (*She jumps up.*)

PHYLLIS

I'll go, Mrs. Gibbons.

(PHYLLIS *runs out of the room.* ETHEL *stands by the fireplace, waiting anxiously. There is the sound of voices in the hall, then* SAM *comes in holding* REG *by the arm.* PHYLLIS *follows them.* REG's *head is bandaged.* ETHEL *gives a cry.*)

ETHEL

Reg! What's happened?

SAM

He's all right, Mrs. Gibbons——

ETHEL

Here, Reg, sit down here, dear.

REG (*sitting down*)

Don't fuss, Mother, I'm all right.

SAM

There was some trouble in the Whitechapel Road, and he got hit by a stone. That was yesterday.

ETHEL

What was he doing in the Whitechapel Road yesterday or any other time?

REG (*smiling a little*)

Hallo, Phyl, what are you doing here?

PHYLLIS

I came over on me bike to find out where you were.

REG

Oh, I see. . . . Thanks.

ETHEL

I've been worrying my heart out about you; you ought to be ashamed of yourself.

(FRANK *comes in, followed by* VI.)

FRANK

Hallo—what's up?

ETHEL

It's Reg, he's been hurt.

SAM

It's nothing serious. I took him to the hospital last night; the doctor said it was only a graze.

VI (*grimly*)

This is all your fault, Sam, you know that, don't you?

FRANK (*going over to* REG)

Shut up a minute, Vi. . . . Feel all right, son?

82

REG (*sullenly*)
Of course I feel all right.

ETHEL
He'd better go up to bed, hadn't he?

FRANK
Leave him where he is a minute.

ETHEL
Don't go for him tonight, Frank, he looks worn out.

FRANK
I'm not going for anybody. I want my supper.
(*He goes to the table and sits down.* ETHEL *takes the bowl of soup from* VI *and serves it to him. She is looking at* REG *anxiously out of the corner of her eye as she does so.* QUEENIE *enters with the toast.*)

VI
You may not be going for anybody, Dad, but I am.

SAM
I think I'll be getting along now.

VI
Not until you've heard what I've got to say, you're not.

REG
Oh, shut up, Vi, what's it got to do with you?

VI
It's all very fine for you to say that nothing serious has happened, Sam, but I should like to remark here and now that it's small thanks to you that it hasn't. You're nothing but a great silly show-off, anyhow, and you've been filling Reg up

83

with your rotten ideas till he can't see straight. Reg thinks you're wonderful—he's younger than you and easily led—but I don't think you're wonderful. I'd think more of you if you did a bit more and talked a bit less. And the next time you come here on a Sunday evening and start pawing me about and saying that Love's the most glorious thing in the world for rich and poor alike, you'll get such a smack in the face that'll make you wish you'd never been born. . . .

SAM
Look here, Vi——

VI
You get out of this house once and for all and don't you show your nose in it again until you've changed your way of thinking. I don't want to have anything to do with a man who listens to a lot of dirty foreigners and goes against his own country. There may be a lot of things wrong, but it's not a noisy great gasbag like you that's going to set them right.

SAM
If that's the way you feel, there isn't anything more to be said.

VI
You're right, dead right, there isn't. Go on, get out! I don't want ever to see you again as long as I live!
(*In silence* SAM *turns and goes out of the room.* VI *waits until she hears the front door slam and then bursts into tears and rushes out into the garden.*)

FRANK
Where's the pepper got to?

QUEENIE

In the sideboard—here—— (*She gets it.*)

ETHEL

Oh dear—I'd better go after her.

FRANK

Much better leave her alone.

REG

Vi hasn't any right to go at Sam like that. What does she know about anything anyway?

FRANK

You keep quiet, son. I'll talk to you presently.

ETHEL

He really ought to go to bed, Frank, he looks that seedy. . . . (*To* REG.) Is your head paining you, dear?

REG (*irritably*)

No, Mum, it's all right, just aching a bit, that's all.

PHYLLIS

I think I'd better be getting back now, Mrs. Gibbons.

ETHEL

Very well, dear, be careful how you go, there's probably a lot of people about tonight.

PHYLLIS

Good night, Queenie.

QUEENIE

Good night, Phyl.

85

PHYLLIS

Good night, Mr. Gibbons.

FRANK

Good night, Phyllis.

PHYLLIS

I hope your head'll be better in the morning, Reg.

REG

Thanks for coming round.

PHYLLIS

Good night.

REG

See you tomorrow?

PHYLLIS

Oh—all right.
(*Phyllis goes out.*)

FRANK (*lighting a cigarette*)

Run out into the garden, Queenie, and fetch Vi in; it's time we was all in bed.

QUEENIE

Righto, Dad. (*She goes into the garden.*)

FRANK

Go on up, Ethel, I'll turn out.

ETHEL

Promise me you won't be hard on him tonight, Frank—look, he's as white as a sheet.

REG (*defiantly*)

I feel fine, Mum, don't worry about me.

86

FRANK

Well, that's good news, anyway.

ETHEL

Come in and say good night to me on your way to bed.

REG

All right.

(ETHEL *stands about helplessly for a moment, and then, one more imploring look at* FRANK, *she goes out of the room.* FRANK *takes a bottle of whisky, a syphon, and two glasses out of the sideboard.*)

FRANK

Feel like a drink, Reg?

REG (*surprised*)

Oh—yes, thanks.

(FRANK *pours two drinks out in silence and takes one over to* REG.)

FRANK

Here you are.

REG (*taking it*)

Thanks, Dad.

FRANK

Here goes. (*He drinks.*)

REG (*also drinking*)

Here goes.

(QUEENIE *and* VI *come in from the garden.* VI *is no longer crying.*)

QUEENIE

Has Mum gone up?

FRANK

Yes, a couple of minutes ago.

QUEENIE

Will you turn out?

FRANK

Yes; you might shut the windows though. Is Percy in all right?

QUEENIE (*shutting the windows*)

Yes, he's asleep in the kitchen.

VI

Good night, Dad.

FRANK (*kissing her*)

Good night, old girl.

QUEENIE (*looking at the table*)

I suppose I'd better clear these things.

FRANK

Leave them for Edie in the morning.

QUEENIE

All right. Good night, Dad.

FRANK (*kissing her*)

Good night, Queenie.

QUEENIE

Good night, Reg.

VI

Good night, Reg.

REG

Good night.

(vi *and* QUEENIE *go out and shut the door after them.*
FRANK *stands leaning against the mantelpiece looking
down at* REG.)

Well, Dad—let's have it and get it over with.

FRANK

Easier said than done. You and me don't quite see things
the same way, do we?

REG

No, I suppose not.

FRANK

That's the trouble, really; it's a pity, too, and I don't see
what there is to be done about it. Got any ideas?

REG

I'm not a kid any more, you know, Dad. I'm growing up
now.

FRANK

Yes, I realise that all right.

REG

I know you think all the things I believe in are wrong. . . .

FRANK

That's where you make a mistake, son. I don't think any
such thing. You've got a right to your opinions the same as
I've got a right to mine. The only thing that worries me is
that you should get it into your head that everybody's

89

against you and, what's more, that all these ideas you've picked up, from Sam and Sam's friends, are new. They're not new, they're as old as the hills. Anybody with any sense has always known about the injustice of some people having a lot and other people having nothing at all, but where I think you go wrong is to blame it all on systems and governments. You've got to go deeper than that to find out the cause of most of the troubles of this world, and when you've had a good look, you'll see likely as not that good old human nature's at the bottom of the whole thing.

REG

If everybody had the same chance as everybody else, human nature'd be better, wouldn't it?

FRANK

It doesn't seem as though we were ever going to find that out, does it? It looks like a bit of a deadlock to me.

REG

As long as we go on admitting that, the workers of the world will go on being ground down and the capitalists will go on fattening on their blood and sweat.

FRANK

Oh, don't let's start all that now, let's use our own words, not other people's.

REG

I don't know what you mean.

FRANK

Oh, come off it, Reg, a kid of your age to be talking about blood and sweat and capitalism! When I was rising twenty

I had a damn sight more cheerful things to think about than
that, I can tell you.

REG

Old people always think that all young people want is to
enjoy themselves.

FRANK

Don't you sit there and tell me you 'aven't been enjoying
yourself tip-top these last few days running about the streets
and throwing stones and yelling your head off. . . .

REG

It's no use talking, Dad, you don't understand, and you
never will.

FRANK

No, you're quite right, arguing never got anybody anywhere; I'll just give you one bit of advice, and then we'll
call it a day. How does that suit?

REG (suspiciously)

What is it?

FRANK

It's this, son. I belong to a generation of men, most of which
aren't here any more, and we all did the same thing for the
same reason, no matter what we thought about politics. Now
all that's over and we're all going on as best as we can as
though nothing had happened. But as a matter of fact, several things did happen and one of them was the country
suddenly got tired; it's tired now. But the old girl's got
stamina and don't you make any mistake about it, and it's
up to us ordinary people to keep things steady. That's your
job, my son, and just you remember it, and the next time

you slam out of the house without a word and never let your mother know where you are and worry her to death, I'll lather the living daylight out of you. Now cut along upstairs and get a bit of sleep.

REG (*rising*)
All right, Dad.

FRANK
And don't forget to go in and say good night to your mum.

REG
All right, Dad—thanks, Dad.
(REG *goes out.* FRANK *looks round the room, finishes his drink, turns out the lights, and follows him as*

THE CURTAIN FALLS.)

ACT TWO

SCENE I

TIME

October, 1931. It is about ten o'clock in the morning.

SCENE

FRANK *is alone in the room finishing his breakfast and read-ing the* Daily Mirror. *He has aged rather during the last six years. His hair is much thinner on the top and his eyes are not what they were, which necessitates his wearing glasses for reading. He is dressed in the trousers and waistcoat of a new pepper-and-salt suit but no coat. He also has a wing collar and a grand grey silk tie and carpet slippers.* QUEENIE, *wrapped in a Japanese silk kimono and with her hair done up in a net, rushes into the room, grabs her handbag off the sideboard, and rushes out again.* FRANK *looks up, stirs his tea thoughtfully, and goes on reading his paper.* EDIE *comes in with a tray.*

During the ensuing scenes there are various sounds of com-motion going on in the house. Scamperings up and down the stairs, doors slamming, bath water running, and occa-sional signs of altercation between members of the family.

EDIE

Mrs. Gibbons said I could clear now so as to give me time to go and dress.

FRANK

Righto, Edie, just leave me with tea.

EDIE (*piling plates onto the tray*)

That bath takes a terrible time to run out; it's my belief the plug hole's stopped up.

FRANK

Better pop round to the tobacconist's and telephone Mr. Freeman.

EDIE

I shan't have time this morning.

FRANK

Tomorrow'll do.

EDIE

Wasn't it awful about poor Mrs. Flint's dress?

FRANK

What happened to it?

EDIE

Percy's been curled up on it all night; covered it with 'airs, he 'as. She nearly 'ad a fit when she found 'im. Wonder you didn't 'ear the noise going on.

FRANK

The whole 'ouse has been in an uproar since eight o'clock.

EDIE

Well, we don't 'ave weddings every day of the week, do we?

FRANK

No, thank God.

96

EDIE (*going out with the tray*)

One thing, we've got a lovely day for it.
(FRANK, *left alone for a moment, goes on with his paper.*
EDIE *returns.*)

D'you mind if I move your tea onto the sideboard a minute?
I'll 'ave to change the cloth.

FRANK

All right—I'll give you a hand.
(*He places the teapot, milk jug, sugar basin, and his cup
on the sideboard and helps* EDIE *to change the tablecloths during the ensuing few lines.*)

EDIE

I went with Mrs. Gibbons to the Plough last night to see
the upstairs room. They've done it up lovely. We 'ad a look
at the cake too; it's ever so pretty. Mrs. Gibbons says I can
'ave a bit to take 'ome to Ernie.

FRANK

Ernie must be getting quite a big boy now.

EDIE

'E's nearly sixteen, but you'd never think it—'e's short like
Dad, you know.

FRANK

Oh, I see.

EDIE

'E started trying to shave himself the other day with Dad's
razor; you'd have died laughing if you'd seen 'im.

FRANK

Did he cut himself?

97

EDIE

Not badly, just took the top off one or two spots.

(EDIE *goes out.* FRANK *puts the tea-things back on the table and sits down again. Presently* BOB MITCHELL *taps at the window.* FRANK *gets up and lets him in.*)

BOB

Well, we've got a nice day for it.

FRANK

Want a cup of tea?

BOB

No, thanks—I'll have a Gold Flake though, if you've got one.

FRANK

There's a packet on the mantelpiece. Chuck us one, too, while you're at it.

(BOB *takes a cigarette himself and throws the packet over to* FRANK, *who misses it.*)

FRANK

Missed it! Can't see a thing with these glasses.

BOB

You'll get used to 'em.

FRANK

How's Nora?

BOB

A bit more cheerful—she always is when Billy's home. One thing, her legs don't pain her any more; she just hasn't got any feeling in 'em at all. The doctor says she won't get no worse nor no better either—just stay about the same.

98

FRANK

Well, as long as she's a bit brighter in herself I suppose we mustn't grumble.

BOB

It was that last miscarriage six years ago that did her in, you know; she'd probably have been all right if it hadn't been for that.

FRANK

Poor old Nora.

BOB

Well, this is a nice conversation for us to be having on the festive day, I will say. How's the happy bridegroom?

FRANK

The happy bridegroom locked himself in the bathroom for nearly an hour this morning; you'd think he hadn't washed for a month.

BOB

Natural anxiety, old man—can't blame 'im!

FRANK

Funny to think of starting off on an 'oneymoon, isn't it? Seems a hell of a long time ago since we did.

BOB

Where did you go for yours?

FRANK

Ramsgate, and it pissed with rain without stopping all the time.

BOB

We went to Swanage—Nora had relatives near there—it was awful.

FRANK

Well, Reg and Phyl ought to enjoy themselves all right. It'll be a change, anyway, going abroad for the first time. I got them special rates all along the line. Even old Baxter himself took a hand.

BOB

Where are they stopping tonight?

FRANK

Dover. Then they get the morning boat and they're in Nice first thing the next day.

BOB

Pretty posh going to the South of France for your honeymoon, nest par?

FRANK

Well, we're only young once.

BOB

You've held that job at Tickler's steady ever since the war, haven't you?

FRANK

Yes, but I nearly lost it once.

BOB

How was that?

FRANK

Well, I'm all right on the business side, you know, travellers' cheques and letters of credit and what not, but once one of our young gentlemen downstairs smashed himself up in a car and I had to go behind the counter for a month—oh dear!—Mr. Baxter sent for me to his office. "Listen, Frank," he says, "there have been complaints. You've issued no less than four sets of tickets to the wrong places inside of the last week through not being able to pronounce the foreign names properly! And as we can't afford to have our customers losing themselves all over the Continent, you'd better go back to your figures!" After that he engaged a couple of ladida young chaps with Oxford accents. You should hear them! I thought one of 'em had swallowed a fishbone the other day, but he was only saying Marseilles!

(SYLVIA *comes hurriedly into the room. She is dressed in a very old wrapper and her head is swathed in a towel. She sees* BOB, *gives a scream of horror, and runs out again. She speaks the ensuing dialogue through the half-open door.*)

SYLVIA

Fancy me coming in looking like this in front of Mr. Mitchell! What will he think?

FRANK

Don't worry. He's broad-minded.

SYLVIA

I had my hair set yesterday and I didn't dare let the damp get to it while I was having my bath.

FRANK

What d'you want, anyway?

101

SYLVIA

Mrs. Flint's feather boa—she says it's in a box on the table by the window—one of its tassels is loose.

FRANK

Hold on a minute. (*He takes a box off the table by the window, brings it to her, and hands it round the door.*) Is this it?

SYLVIA

Yes, that's it—thanks. (*She goes.*)

FRANK (*shuts the door and comes back into the room*) This house has been a fair circus all the morning, I give you my word.

BOB

Reg is doing all right, isn't he now?

FRANK

Yes, he got his raise. He's assistant clerk to one of the managers.

BOB

No more of that Bolshie nonsense?

FRANK

Oh no, he's got quite a lot of horse sense, you know, underneath. He had a nice look at the Labour Government and saw what a mess they was making of everything. You should have heard him the other night when the election results came through—jumping up and down like a jack-in-the-box, he was. He's Britain for ever now all right.

BOB

Well, that's good news.

FRANK

Sam shook him a bit too, you know, giving up that old Bombshell Bookshop of his and marrying Vi and settling down. Oh yes, we've all gone back to being the backbone of the Empire.

(REG *comes in in his shirt sleeves. He carries two ties in his hand.*)

REG

Dad—— (*He sees* BOB.) Oh, hallo, Uncle Bob.

BOB

Hallo, Reg—feeling nervous?

REG (*grinning*)

My legs feel a bit funny. Is Billy nearly ready?

BOB

Yes, and he's got the ring all right too. I saw him put it in his pocket myself. He'll be here in a minute.

REG

Which tie d'you think, Dad? The bow, or the long one?

FRANK

Let's have a look. (*He holds them both up.*) Try the bow, it looks more dressy.

REG (*tying the bow in front of the glass on the mantelpiece*)

Aunt Sylvia's been having a good cry upstairs.

FRANK

What about?

103

REG

Oh, first of all, she said she felt seedy and that weddings always upset her anyhow, then Granny flew at her and said if only she'd had the sense to get married herself we should all have been saved a lot of trouble!

FRANK

I don't know how those two would get on without each other, and that's a fact.

BOB

I'll be getting along now and get myself spruced up for the happy moment.

FRANK

Righto.

BOB

See you at the church, Reg.

REG

You might tell Billy to get a move on, Uncle Bob.

BOB

I will.

(BOB *goes out.* FRANK *sits down in the armchair and looks thoughtfully at* REG.)

FRANK

Well, son!

REG

Well, Dad!

104

FRANK

I suppose I ought to be giving you a few bits of fatherly advice by rights.

REG (*blandly*)

What about, Dad?

FRANK

Well, there's the facts of life, for instance.

REG

I could probably tell you a few things about them.

FRANK

I bet you could at that. (*There is a pause.*) Reg——

REG (*solemnly*)

Yes, Dad?

FRANK

And I'll trouble you to wipe that innocent look off your face before I say what I've got to say.

REG

What have you got to say, Dad?

FRANK

That's right, make the whole thing easy for me.

REG

I don't know what you're talking about.

FRANK

I'm not talking about anything yet.

REG

All right—fire away.

FRANK (*with an effort*)

Would you say—taken by and large—that you'd been a good boy on the whole—since you've grown up?

REG

Depends what you mean by good.

FRANK

You know what I mean all right, so don't talk so soft.

REG

Women?

FRANK

Yes.

REG

Oh, I've had my bits of fun every now and again.

FRANK

Never got yourself into any sort of trouble, have you, without telling me?

REG

No, Dad.

FRANK

Marriage is a bit different, you know, from just—having a bit of fun.

REG (*fidgeting*)

Yes—I expect it is.

FRANK

Women aren't all the same by any manner of means. Some of them don't care what happens so long as they have a good time; marriage isn't important to them beyond having

106

the ring and being called Mrs. Whatever it is. But your mother wasn't that sort and I don't think Phyllis is either. She's a nice girl and she loves you a lot.

REG

I know, Dad.

FRANK

And when a woman loves you that much she's liable to be a bit over-sensitive, you know. It's as well to remember that.

REG

I'll remember, Dad.

FRANK

Just go carefully with her—be gentle. You've got a long time to be together, all your lives, I hope. It's worth while to go easy and get to know each other gradual. And if later on, a long time later on, you ever get yourself caught up with someone else, just see to it that Phyllis doesn't get hurt by it. Put your wife first always. Lots of little things can happen on the side without doing much harm, providing you don't make a fool of yourself and keep quiet about it. But anything that's liable to bust up your home and your life with your wife and children's not worth it. Just remember that and you won't go far wrong.

REG

All right, Dad—thanks a lot.

FRANK

I only hope you'll have the luck I've had. I can't say more than that, can I?

107

REG

No, Dad.

FRANK

Well, I'd better be getting myself dressed up. So long, son.
(*He rather clumsily puts his arms round* REG *for a minute and goes out of the room.* REG, *left alone, takes a
cigarette out of the packet on the table, lights it, and
then returns to the glass and scrutinises his face in it.*
BILLY *enters through the french window. He has grown
matured and set with the years. He is now wearing the
uniform of a Petty Officer.*)

BILLY

Don't worry, old man—you look gorgeous.

REG (*turning*)

Oh, it's you, is it?

BILLY

All ready for the ball and chain?

REG

You're too bloody cheerful by half.

BILLY

Of course I am. I'm a sailor, aren't I? All sailors are bright
and breezy; it's in the regulations.

REG

You must be the life and soul of your ship.

BILLY (*helping himself to a cigarette*)

Oh, I am, I am. Only the other morning the Admiral sent for
me. "Mitchell," he said, "make me laugh." So I told him the
one about the parrot. "Mitchell," he said, "the ship's yours."

"What'll I do with it?" I said. "Scuttle it," he said, and cut his throat from ear to ear.

REG

Have you got the ring all right?

BILLY

Well, as a matter of fact, I dropped it down the whatsit, but don't worry, we sent for a plumber.

REG

I'd better go and get my coat; we'll have to be starting in a minute.

BILLY

Righto.
(*On his way out he bangs into* QUEENIE *coming in.* QUEENIE *is wearing a blue bridesmaid's dress and hat and is carrying a bunch of flowers.*)

QUEENIE

Why can't you look where you're going? You nearly knocked me down.

REG

Sorry, old girl——
(*He goes out.* QUEENIE *sees* BILLY.)

QUEENIE

Oh, it's you.

BILLY

Yes. (*He turns away.*)

QUEENIE

Well, it's a nice day, anyhow, isn't it?

109

BILLY

Fine.

QUEENIE (*puts her flowers on the sideboard and comes over to him*)

You haven't said anything to Reg, have you? You haven't said anything to anyone?

BILLY

Of course not.

QUEENIE (*looking down*)

I'm awfully sorry about last night, Billy, really I am.

BILLY

No need to be sorry, it's not your fault.

QUEENIE

When you've gone back, they'll all be asking me questions— I don't know what to say.

BILLY (*not looking at her*)

Tell 'em the truth. I love you and asked you to marry me. You don't love me and said no. It's simple enough.

QUEENIE

It sounds horrid when you say it like that.

BILLY

No use pretending, is there?

QUEENIE

No, I suppose there isn't. I am sorry, though, all the same; you do believe that, don't you?

BILLY

Yes, I believe it all right.

110

QUEENIE

I never did say I would, did I? I mean I never let you think——

BILLY

I'm not blaming you, I told you that last night. I just can't help feeling a bit low—that's natural enough, isn't it?

QUEENIE

I suppose you won't write to me any more now, will you?

BILLY

You're a funny girl, I must say.

QUEENIE

I don't see anything so very funny about that.

BILLY

You want everything, don't you?

QUEENIE

It's unkind to talk like that.

BILLY

You know I love you more than anyone else and want to marry you, don't you? You've always known that anyway. You turn me down flat and then want me to go on writing to you. What shall I have to write about to you any more? If you've taken the trouble to read my letters up to date you might remember they was mostly about the future and what fun we were going to have when we were together. All that's gone now, hasn't it? I'll send you a weather report every so often if you like.

QUEENIE

If you're going to turn nasty about it there's no use saying any more.

BILLY

There's someone else, isn't there?

QUEENIE

I don't know what you mean.

BILLY

I mean what I say. You're in love with someone else, aren't you?

QUEENIE

It's no business of yours if I am.

BILLY

It's true though, isn't it?

QUEENIE

Now look here, Billy——

BILLY

Why couldn't you have told me last night, or a long time ago? Don't you trust me?

QUEENIE

You haven't got any right to ask me things like that.

BILLY

Listen here, Queenie. You've been the only girl I've cared a damn about for getting on seven years now. We haven't seen much of each other on account of me being away at sea, but you've known all the time that I was thinking of you and hoping that as the years went by you'd grow out of some of

112

your highfalutin ideas and think me good enough to be your husband. All that gives me the right to ask you anything I like——

QUEENIE

No, it doesn't.

BILLY

Is there someone else or isn't there?

QUEENIE

Yes, there is, if you must know. So there!

BILLY

Are you going to marry him?

QUEENIE

If you say a word about this to anyone I'll never speak to you again as long as I live.

BILLY

Are you going to marry him?

QUEENIE

No.

BILLY

Why not?

QUEENIE

That's my affair.

BILLY

Is he married already?

QUEENIE

I wish you'd leave me alone.

113

BILLY

Is he?

QUEENIE

Yes, he is! Now are you satisfied?

BILLY (*turning away*)

Oh, Queenie, you're an awful fool—I do wish you weren't.

QUEENIE

Who are you calling a fool? People can't help their feelings.

BILLY

No, but they can have enough sense not to let their feelings
get the better of them. What you're doing's wrong which-
ever way you look at it. There's your mother and father to
start with; it'll break their hearts if ever they find out about
it. Then there's the man's wife, whoever she is; you're laying
up trouble there. But most important of all, there's you. You
won't get much out of it in the long run and don't you fool
yourself. You're not that kind of girl really, whatever you
may think. It looks to me as if you're on the way to mucking
things up all round for yourself and everyone else——

QUEENIE

Thanks very much for the lecture.

BILLY

You're quite right. It's no good me saying any more. I'll go
up and talk to Reg. Good-bye and good luck.

(*He goes quickly out of the room.* QUEENIE *stands still
for a moment, looking after him, biting her lip. She
looks, just for a second, as though she might be going to
cry, then she tosses her head and, turning to the glass,
begins to fiddle about with her hat.* ETHEL *comes in, fol-*

lowed by FRANK. ETHEL *is elaborately dressed in grey silk.* FRANK *has enhanced the glory of his pepper-and-salt suit by the addition of a large white buttonhole and some obviously new boots.*)

ETHEL

Vi and Sam ought to be here by now—I wonder where they are.

FRANK (*to* QUEENIE)

Been talking to Billy?

QUEENIE

Yes. He's upstairs with Reg.

FRANK (*sitting down*)

These boots are giving me what for all right. If they're like this now, what are they going to be like by the evening?

QUEENIE

A couple of weddings in one year is a bit too much of a good thing if you ask me.

FRANK

Well, here's hoping you get off soon and make the third.

QUEENIE

I wish you wouldn't say things like that, Dad, it sounds so vulgar.

FRANK

Very sorry, I'm sure.

QUEENIE

When I marry, if I ever do, it will be in a registry office anyway—all this commotion.

FRANK

Your mother wouldn't like that—would you, Ethel?

ETHEL

I certainly would not.

QUEENIE

I shouldn't let you know. I shouldn't let anybody know. I'd do it on the quiet. I don't like to think of everyone staring at me and making remarks.

ETHEL

I never heard such nonsense.

FRANK

Our Queenie has ideas of her own, Ethel, or anyway she thinks they're her own.

QUEENIE

I'll never be a bridesmaid again anyhow as long as I live. Look at this dress—and the hat.

ETHEL

You've done something to it, haven't you?

QUEENIE

You bet I have. I wouldn't have worn it as it was.

ETHEL

You'll look different from all the others.

QUEENIE

So I should hope.

ETHEL

Marjorie will be upset. She and Phyl took such a lot of trouble——

116

QUEENIE

They don't know anything about clothes, either of them. Thank heavens none of the girls at the shop can see me looking such a sight.

FRANK

It seems to me they must be a pretty fancy lot, them girls at your shop! We're always being told what they like and what they don't like.

QUEENIE

All right, Dad, there's no need for you to be sarcastic.

ETHEL

Don't snap at your father, Queenie. I don't know what's come over you lately.

QUEENIE (*with an edge on her voice*)

Nothing's come over me—I just don't like looking common.

FRANK

I shouldn't worry about that if I was you—it can't be helped. After all, according to some people's standards, I suppose you are common.

ETHEL

Frank, how can you say such a thing! She's nothing of the sort.

FRANK

It's your mother's fault really, you know. She caught me on the 'op! I was all set to marry a duchess when along she come and busted up the whole thing with her fatal charm. And what's more, the duchess never forgave me. That's why I haven't set foot inside Buckingham Palace these last thirty years.

117

QUEENIE

You think you're very funny, don't you, Dad?

FRANK

I think you're the one that's funny, if you must know.

QUEENIE

Why, what have I done?

FRANK

It isn't what you've done, my girl, it's what you're trying
to do.

QUEENIE

And what's that, may I ask?

FRANK

You're trying to be something you're not. There's nothing
funnier than that. To see you flouncing about and putting
on airs just because you happen to have polished Lady Kiss-
me-quick's nails is enough to make a cat laugh.

QUEENIE (*angrily*)

You don't believe in people trying to better themselves, do
you? Just because you're content to stick in the same place
all your life and do your bit of gardening on Saturday after-
noons in your shirt sleeves——

ETHEL

Don't you dare speak to your father like that!

QUEENIE

Living in a suburb and doing your own cooking and washing
up may be good enough for you, but it isn't good enough for
me. I'm sick of this house and everybody in it, and I'm not
going to stand it much longer, you see——

ETHEL

You're a wicked, ungrateful girl and you ought to be ashamed of yourself.

QUEENIE

Well, I'm not, so there!

ETHEL

If it wasn't for being Reg's wedding day I'd lock you in your room till you came to your senses.

FRANK

Well, a few years ago we had Reg nagging at us because we were living on the fat of the land while the poor workers was starving. Now we have Queenie turning on us because we're not good enough for her. I don't know what's wrong with our children, Ethel, my girl. Seems to me Vi's the only one who's got any real sense.

QUEENIE

Vi! Vi's different from me—can't you see—she always has been! She doesn't like the things I like or want the things I want. She's perfectly happy in that mangy little flat, doing her own housework and making her own clothes. She likes bossing Sam too. Why, he's a changed man since he married her.

ETHEL

And a good job too.

QUEENIE

It seems to me that all the spirit's gone out of him. He's just like anybody else now—just respectable.

119

FRANK

Well, what's the matter with that?

QUEENIE

Oh, nothing. What's the use of arguing! You don't understand what I'm talking about.

FRANK

Don't waste your breath on us then, Queenie. We're as we are and that's how we're going to stay, and if you don't like it you can lump it. One of these days when you know a bit more, you'll find out that there are worse things than being ordinary and respectable and living the way you've been brought up to live. In the meantime—as long as you're with us, I mean—your mum and me'd be much obliged if you'd keep your tongue between your teeth and behave yourself. Now you'd better go upstairs, slap some more paint on your face, make yourself look as much like a tart as possible, and do the girls at the shop credit. Go on—'op it!

QUEENIE

Thanks very much—I will! (*She flounces out of the room and slams the door.*)

ETHEL

There now. She'll be snapping our heads off for the rest of the day.

FRANK

We spoilt her when she was little. We've always spoilt her.

ETHEL

No, Frank, it isn't only that. She's upset about something—sort of strung up—she has been for a long time. I wish I knew what it was.

FRANK

You mean you think she's in some sort of trouble?

ETHEL

I don't know what to think. When Billy came back last year and they went out together nearly every evening, I thought everything was going to be all right; then they had words—I don't know what about, I'm sure—and off he went.

FRANK

Don't worry, old girl, it'll all come out in the wash.

(EDIE, *resplendent in a green dress and hat, rushes in.*)

EDIE

The car's come. It looks ever so nice all done up with white ribbons.

FRANK

Good! Let's have a look, Ethel. You'd better call Reg, Edie— tell him it's here.

(EDIE *runs out.* FRANK *takes* ETHEL *by the hand and they go out into the hall and apparently open the front door because they can be heard making exclamations of approval of the car.* REG *and* BILLY *come clattering down the stairs and into the room.* REG *is palpably nervous.*)

REG

I suppose we ought to be starting, oughtn't we?

BILLY

Yes, it's about time now; it wouldn't do for the blushing bride to get there before we do.

(FRANK *and* ETHEL *return.*)

121

ETHEL

Have you seen the car? Mr. Stevens has done it up lovely!

REG

Yes, we saw it drive up.

FRANK

Feeling nervous, son?

REG

Yes, a bit.

ETHEL (*emotionally*)

Oh, Reg!

REG

Cheer up, Mother.

ETHEL (*fumbling for her handkerchief*)

I can't hardly believe it—it seems only the other day that——

REG (*putting his arm round her*)

All right, Mum, we know all about that. I was a little toddler cutting me first teeth and look at me now, a great grown man——

FRANK

Don't start getting weepy now, Ethel; it's a wedding, not a funeral!

ETHEL

Oh, hold your noise, Frank, and be quiet.

REG (*kissing her*)

See you at the church, Mum. Cheero, Dad—come on, Billy.

FRANK

Cheero, son—don't forget to send the car straight back.

BILLY

I'll see to that—it'll be back in five minutes.

ETHEL

Have you said good-bye to your granny and Auntie Syl?

REG

Yes—I saw them upstairs.

BILLY (*sternly*)

Come *on*.

REG

All right. Good-bye all——

(*He and* BILLY *go out.* ETHEL *sinks into a chair and weeps a little.*)

FRANK

Come off it, Ethel, there's nothing to cry about.

ETHEL

I can't help it.

FRANK

You'll make your nose red.

ETHEL

I don't care if I do. He's our only son, isn't he? And he's going away from us, isn't he? That's enough to make any woman cry.

FRANK

Well, they'll be back from the honeymoon in two weeks and living just round the corner——

123

ETHEL

It's all very fine for you—you didn't bring him into the world and hold him at your breast——

FRANK

I should have looked a proper fool if I had.

ETHEL

You don't know anything about it; you haven't got any feelings.

FRANK (*comforting her*)

Come on now—shut up crying and put your hat straight.

(SYLVIA *comes in leading* MRS. FLINT *by the arm.* SYLVIA *is wearing an artistic confection of brown and orange, also a necklace of thick amber beads.* MRS. FLINT *is in purple satin and a black flowered hat. She is led to her chair and settles herself in it.*)

MRS. F.

If I could lay my hands on that cat I'd kill it. Half an hour it took me to pick the hairs off, and the front of the skirt all creased too.

SYLVIA

It doesn't show.

MRS. F. (*looking balefully at* SYLVIA)

Is that the new hat we've heard such a lot about?

SYLVIA

Yes, it is.

MRS. F. (*grunting*)

Oh!

SYLVIA

Why, is there anything the matter with it?

ETHEL (*peaceably*)

I think it's very nice, don't you, Frank?

FRANK

It looks fine.

MRS. F.

There's something a bit funny about the crown, isn't there?

SYLVIA

I don't know what you mean.

MRS. F.

Well, of course, if you're satisfied . . .

ETHEL

Do be quiet, Mother. Don't take any notice of her, Sylvia.

MRS. F.

That'll be no change. Nobody ever does take any notice of me. But old as I am, I can at least get myself to the church on me feet, which is more than can be said for Phyllis's aunt, who has to be wheeled in.

SYLVIA

She's bedridden, poor woman.

MRS. F.

I shouldn't be surprised if she could walk as well as anybody if she liked.

(VI *and* SAM *come in.* QUEENIE *follows them.* SAM *has improved with the years. He is neatly dressed and wears an air of respectability which was lacking before.* VI *looks very assured and smart in a pink dress and hat.*)

125

VI

The front door was open, so we came straight in.

ETHEL (*kissing her*)
Why, Vi, how pretty you look, dear.

VI (*showing off her dress*)
I only finished it at eleven o'clock last night.

SAM
The whole flat's been covered in paper patterns and bits of stuff and pins for the last ten days. Has Reg gone?

FRANK
Yes, he and Billy went about two minutes ago. They're sending the car straight back.

QUEENIE
I hope they'll get a move on. I've got to be on time to meet Marjorie and Doreen and Amy Weaver.

VI
It does look nice, that dress, doesn't it, Sam?

SAM
Very nice indeed.

QUEENIE
I think it's awful.

VI
Oh, you always say that, Queenie; it was exactly the same at my wedding.
(BOB MITCHELL *comes in through the french window.*)

BOB
Hallo, Vi—hallo, Sam—car come back yet?

ETHEL

Tell Edie to keep an eye out for it, Queenie.

QUEENIE (*going to door and shouting through it*)
Edie—keep a lookout for the car—you'd better stay by the drawing-room window.

EDIE (*off*)
All right.

MRS. F.

On my wedding day there was a thunderstorm and a man got struck by lightning just opposite the church.

FRANK
That must have cheered things up.

MRS. F.
One side of his face was all twisted.

QUEENIE
Why, Granny, did you stop in the middle of the service and pop out to have a look?

MRS. F.
We did not, and I'll thank you, miss, not to be saucy.

QUEENIE
Saucy indeed—what a way to talk.

FRANK
I'm surprised at you, Mother, I am really, using such expressions in front of our Queenie. You know she meets all the best people nowadays.

QUEENIE
Oh, shut up, Dad.

127

FRANK

Better sit down, hadn't we, all of us? No sense in standing about.

ETHEL (*looking at the clock*)

It ought to be back by now.

FRANK

Don't fuss, Ethel.

MRS. F. (*reminiscently*)

It seems only yesterday.

ETHEL

What does, Mother?

MRS. F.

The day you and Frank married. I can see your poor aunt Connie now coughing her heart out in the vestry. It was only three months after that she was taken.

FRANK (*cheerfully*)

That's right. (*He winks at* BOB.)

MRS. F.

I'll be lucky if I last out another year.

FRANK

Oh dear, oh dear!

MRS. F. (*darkly*)

I don't suppose anybody'd mind much—there's many as might say it was a blessing in disguise, I shouldn't wonder.

FRANK

Now then, Mother—none of that.

MRS. F.

Dr. Spearman said my heart was thoroughly worn out ever since that bronchitis I 'ad in February.

SYLVIA (*contemptuously*)

Dr. Spearman!

MRS. F.

He's a better man than your Dr. Lewis any day of the week. If it hadn't been for him having presence of mind Mrs. Spooner would be dead as a doornail at this very minute.

SYLVIA

That's what you say.

MRS. F.

Eleven o'clock she was doing her shopping and she was putting the joint in the oven at twelve—a nice bit of leg of lamb it was too—and at half-past one she was in the 'ospital lying flat on 'er back on the operating table—and if it hadn't been for Dr. Spearman——

ETHEL

I wonder what's happened to that car—it's getting on, you know.

BOB

Shall I go out and have a look?

FRANK

No—Edie's watching out for it.

ETHEL

I suppose Billy remembered to tell the driver all right. He's a new man, you know, not the same one we had for Vi's wedding. He might not have understood.

FRANK

Well, if it comes to the pinch we can walk anyway, can't we? It's only just up the road.

SAM

Vi oughtn't to do much walking.

VI

Don't be silly, Sam. It's weeks away yet.

SAM

All the same, it's silly to go taking risks.

FRANK (*at door, shouting*)
Any signs yet, Edie?

EDIE

No. . . . (*She appears.*) Mrs. Baker and Miss Whitney just come out of number twelve—you should see 'em—got up to kill, they are.

SYLVIA

That Miss Whitney—stuck-up thing!

ETHEL

Well, she'll have to sit next to Mr. Bolton at the table whether she likes it or not.

FRANK

Go back to the front room, Edie.

QUEENIE

Don't hang out of the window, though, it looks silly.

EDIE (*reproachfully*)
As if I would! (*She goes.*)

130

SYLVIA

I had those pains again in the night, Ethel, something terrible they were—started about two o'clock.

MRS. F.

It's all those sweets you eat. There's nothing like sweets for
giving you wind.

SYLVIA

It was *not* wind!

QUEENIE

It's nearly ten to—I think I'd better go on in a minute.

FRANK

I wish everybody'd stop fussing. It gives me the pip.

ETHEL

It shouldn't have taken Reg and Billy more than three or
four minutes to get there.

MRS. F.

I'm sure I hope nothing dreadful's happened to them.

VI

Oh, Granny, what could have?

MRS. F.

Accidents will happen.

QUEENIE

Well, they can't have been struck by lightning anyhow.

SYLVIA

I shouldn't think there was the chance of many accidents
just between here and St. Michael's.

131

MRS. F.

Well, you never know.

FRANK (*irritably*)

All right, all right, have it your own way. There's been a terrible accident, the wedding's off. Reg 'as got concussion and we're all going to spend the rest of the day yelling our eyes out! How's that?

SYLVIA

Some people seem to think of nothing but horrors; it's morbid, that's what it is.

MRS. F.

I'll thank you not to call me names, Sylvia Gibbons.

SYLVIA

You make me tired.

ETHEL

Don't answer back, Sylvia, it'll only mean a row.

SYLVIA

I'm sure I don't want to say anything to anybody, but really——

MRS. F.

Pity you don't keep quiet then!

SYLVIA (*losing her temper*)

Who are you to talk to me like that? I've had about enough of your nagging——

FRANK

Shut UP, Sylvia.

VI

You know it's no good arguing with her, Auntie Syl.

SYLVIA (*violently*)

I don't know any such thing. I tell you I'm sick of it—morning, noon, and night it's the same thing—she's at me all the time, and I won't stand it. I've got as much right to be in this house as she has; just because she's old and pretends her heart's weak she thinks she can say what she likes, but I'll tell you one thing here and now, and that is that I've had enough trouble and sorrow and suffering in my life to put up with her eternal nagging and nasty insinuations. She's nothing but a spiteful, mischief-making old cat, and if I have any more of it, old as she is, I'll slap her face till her teeth rattle!

(SYLVIA *bursts into violent hysterical tears.* MRS. FLINT, *with a cry of rage, struggles up from her chair.* FRANK *and* BOB *endeavour to calm her.* ETHEL *and* VI *and* SAM *help* SYLVIA, *sobbing, into a chair.* QUEENIE *regards the proceedings with obvious contempt. Everybody talks at once.* EDIE *rushes in from the hall.*)

EDIE (*excitedly—above the din*)

It's here—it's here—the car's here.

(*The general noise dies down into silence.* SYLVIA's *sobs subside. Everyone straightens themselves.*)

FRANK (*quietly*)

Come on, Mother—it's time to go to the church.

VI

Come on, Granny—come with me.

MRS. F.

I'm all right.

133

VI (*coaxingly*)
You'd better, dear; you know what you are and it's quite a long service——

FRANK
Take her to the outside one, Vi, there's no need to trail all the way upstairs.

(VI *leads* MRS. FLINT, *still protesting, out of the room.* BOB *goes out with* SYLVIA, *who is making gallant efforts to control herself.* SAM, QUEENIE, *and* EDIE *follow them.* FRANK *looks at* ETHEL *and laughs, then he slips his arm through hers—as they go.*)

FRANK
Come on, old girl. . . .

THE LIGHTS FADE.

SCENE II

TIME

November, 1931. It is about midnight.

SCENE

The room is empty and the door into the hall open.
The stage is dark except for a glow from the dying fire.
Presently QUEENIE *can be seen tiptoeing down the stairs. She*
is wearing a hat and coat and carrying a small suitcase. She
puts this down just inside the door, switches on the light,
goes, still on tiptoe, over to the fireplace, and props a letter
up on the mantelpiece. Then, with a hurried look round, she
switches off the light again and goes out into the hall, taking
her suitcase with her. The front door is heard to open and
close softly.
There is a slight pause. The clock on the mantelpiece strikes
twelve. There is a scuffling noise at the window; it opens
and the curtains blow out in the draught. BOB'S *voice is*
heard to say "Oh dear!" He comes in, followed by FRANK.
They are both in ordinary suits but wearing their war
medals. They are also both a little bit drunk.

FRANK

God help poor sailors on a night like this!

BOB

Where's the light?

FRANK (*fastening the window*)

Over by the door. Lucky this was open, we'd have woke up Ethel if we'd of come in by the front.

BOB (*switching on the light*)

'Ere we are.

FRANK

Better shut that door while you're at it.

BOB

Righto. (*He shuts it.*)

FRANK

Now then.

BOB

Now then what?

FRANK (*at the sideboard*)

One more nightcap.

BOB

You won't half have a thick head in the morning!

FRANK (*producing whisky and glasses*)

What about you?

BOB

I'm past caring, old man.

FRANK

That's right—say when—— (*He pours out the whisky.*)

136

BOB

Here, go easy.

FRANK

'Old it while I put the soda in.

BOB (*taking the glass*)

Your eyes look terrible! All swimmy.

FRANK

Never you mind about my eyes—yours don't look so good from here! (*He squirts the syphon violently, splashing them both.*)

BOB

Look out!

FRANK

Oh dear! Now I've wetted me Victoria Cross.

BOB

Don't you wish you had one?

FRANK

Fat lot of good it'd do me if I 'ad.
(*The pouring out of the drinks having been accomplished, he holds up his glass.*)
I would like to take this opportunity of saying that my old regiment's the finest in the world. Tonight we have all here present been united in friendship and memory.

BOB

You'll wake up your missus in a minute and she'll unite you with a slap in the chops for coming home tiddley!

137

FRANK (*ignoring him, swaying slightly*)

When I see before me all these well-remembered faces and recall, with a tug of the 'eartstrings, the hardships and perils we endured together——

BOB

Now listen, old man, I've heard all this once already tonight, you know——

FRANK (*sternly*)

Don't interrupt! My old regiment's the finest in the world——

BOB

Next to the East Surreys it is.

FRANK

Here's to the Buffs! (*He drinks.*)

BOB

Here's to the East Surreys!

FRANK (*affectionately*)

The East Surreys is the finest regiment in the world too——

BOB

That's right.

FRANK (*drinking*)

Here's to the East Surreys!

BOB (*drinking*)

Here's to the Buffs!

FRANK (*sitting down at the table*)

What was that one that chap told us about the couple in the park?

138

BOB (*also sitting*)

You mean the one when the copper comes up and starts arguing and the woman says——

FRANK

No, no, no, not that one—the one when the man says to the girl—what was it now? You've gone and put it clean out of me head.

BOB

You don't mean the one the little bald bloke with glasses told us?

FRANK

No, no, no—that was the one about the woman in the bath when the 'ouse caught on fire—bloody funny it was too, I will say. (*He starts to laugh.*)

BOB

Oh, shut up, you'll start me off. (*He laughs.*)

FRANK (*wiping his eyes*)

That little bastard can tell 'em all right and no mistake about it——

BOB (*convulsed*)

It wasn't what he said so much as the way he said it—dry, you know, that's what he was—dry——

FRANK

That reminds me—— (*He rises and goes to the whisky bottle.*)

BOB

Here, 'old on, old cock—I got to get home——

139

FRANK

I'll see you home and then, and then'll we'll have one more with you.

BOB

I suppose there's nothing to eat, is there?

FRANK (*pouring fresh drinks*)

'Ave a look in the sideboard.

BOB (*on his knees at the sideboard cupboard*)

There's a cruet and some A1 Sauce—here we are—biscuits—— (*He produces an opened tin of Huntley and Palmer's.*)

FRANK

There ought to be some fish paste by rights.

BOB (*groping in the cupboard*)

Oh, blast! I stuck me finger in the jam!

FRANK (*crouching down*)

Here—let me have a look. (*After a moment he produces a bottle of bloater paste and the A1 Sauce. He puts them on the table.*)

BOB (*admiringly*)

That's fine.

FRANK

The butter's in the larder, so we'd better do without it—Sylvia sleeps just over the kitchen and she's got ears like a hawk. We can spread the paste on the biscuits and put a bit of A1 on top to pep it up.

140

BOB
It ought to sit nicely on that dinner we had! Where's a
knife?

FRANK
In the drawer.
(BOB *finds a knife in the drawer and they both sit down
again at the table.*)

BOB (*holding up his glass*)
Huntley and Palmer! (*He drinks.*)

FRANK (*doing the same*)
Crosse and Blackwell—God bless 'em! (*He drinks.*)

BOB (*giggling*)
We shan't half look silly if Ethel catches us.

FRANK
It's me own house, isn't it? I can do what I like in it. An
Englishman's home is his castle.

BOB (*proffering the bloater paste*)
Here, smell that a minute.

FRANK
What's the matter with it?

BOB
Seems a bit off to me.

FRANK (*smelling it*)
No—don't be so fancy—it's only the rubber round the top.

BOB (*accepting the explanation*)
All right, all right—I only wondered.

141

FRANK

Heard from Billy lately?

BOB

Yes—he writes once a week—he's in Malta now.

FRANK

Good old Billy! He's a fine boy.

BOB

So's Reg.

FRANK (*raising his glass*)

Here's to 'em both. Our sons!

BOB (*doing the same*)

Our sons!
(*They both drink.*)

FRANK

Seems sort of funny, doesn't it?

BOB

What does?

FRANK

Getting old.

BOB

Yes, you're a grandfather! Think of that.

FRANK

I wish it had been a boy instead of a girl, Vi's kid, still there's lots of time yet.

BOB

I suppose Reg and Phyl will be having one soon?

FRANK

Well, he's got a Baby Austin already! (*He laughs delightedly at his own joke.*)

BOB (*also laughing*)

He come to the office in it the other day—I saw him out of Mr. Freedman's window. Drove up as if he owned the street, he did.

FRANK

Mr. Freedman likes him, doesn't he?

BOB

Of course he does. Everybody likes Reg; he's the most popular chap in the office.

FRANK

Is he really?

BOB

You bet he is.

FRANK (*almost painfully pleased*)

That's good, isn't it?

BOB

You know, I've never said much about it, but I always thought that maybe Billy and Queenie might—one day——

FRANK

Oh, Queenie gives me a headache—all her airs and graces—a good hiding is what she needs.

BOB

That wouldn't be any use—some girls get like that—no doing anything with them.

143

FRANK (*patting* BOB'S *arm affectionately*)

Listen, Bob, old man. I want exactly what you want, see? I've wanted Queenie and Billy to get together ever since they were kids. I'd rather have Billy in the family than anyone else in the world, and that's a fact—you know that, don't you?

BOB

Of course I do.

FRANK

But it's no use trying to drive people the way they don't want to go.

BOB

I think Billy'd stand by her always, whatever she did.

FRANK (*almost sharply*)

How d'you mean?

BOB

I don't know—I just mean he loves her, that's all.

FRANK

Funny, isn't it, about having children and seeing what they grow up like? There's Vi, for instance. I've never had a moment's worry about her since the day she was born, always behaves nicely, always good to her mother——

BOB

Nothing the matter with Vi.

FRANK

Then there's Queenie—as different from her as chalk from cheese. She's a fine girl, too, in some ways; she's got more go than Vi, you know, and smart! Whew! Always was, even

144

when she was little—that's what makes her a bit hard to manage now, you know—she's too quick for us.

BOB

Reg is the one for my money.

FRANK (*smiling*)

Now you're talking. . . .
(*They sit in silence for a moment, looking back over the years.*)

BOB

Well, it's a strange world and no mistake. I was thinking that tonight, looking at all those chaps in your regiment—wondering what they were feeling like. Some of 'em looked all right, of course, but some looked a bit under the weather.

FRANK

We've been lucky.

BOB

You've said it.

FRANK

I wonder when the next war'll be.

BOB

Not in our time, nor in our sons' time, thank God!

FRANK

I wouldn't bank on that.

BOB

How could there be? Everybody's disarming.

FRANK

We are.

145

BOB

There's the good old League of Nations.

FRANK

It don't seem able to have stopped Japan turning nasty.

BOB

Japan! Who cares about Japan? It's a nice long way off for one thing.

FRANK

Lots of trouble can start from a long way off.

BOB

Oh, don't you worry your head about Japan.

FRANK (*thoughtfully*)

Of course I know if they really start behaving badly all we got to do is to send a couple of battleships along and scare the little sods out of their wits.

BOB

That's right.

FRANK

All the same——

BOB

We've got the finest Navy in the world and don't you forget it.

FRANK

As long as we treat it right.

BOB

How d'you mean?

146

FRANK
What about Invergordon?

BOB
That wasn't the Navy's fault.

FRANK
I never said it was.

BOB
Well, then!

FRANK
It was the fault of the old men at the top. It always is the fault of the old men at the top. They're the ones that muck things up. We can't afford to have much more of that sort of thing, you know.

BOB
Well, we've got a brand-new Government now and everything in the garden's lovely.

FRANK (*raising the glass*)
Here's hoping!

BOB
Chuck us another biscuit.

FRANK (*pushing the tin towards him*)
Here. . . .

BOB
I'll have to be pushing off home in a minute.

FRANK
Finish up and have one more before you go.

147

BOB

Now listen, Frankie boy, we're up to the gills already.

FRANK (*at the sideboard*)

Just a little one for the road.

BOB

The road? I only got about three yards to go.

FRANK

We don't have a binge like this every day of the week.

BOB (*making a dive at him*)

Here, that's enough. (*He catches* FRANK's *arm to prevent him pouring out too much, causing him to drop the bottle on the floor with a crash.*)

FRANK

Now you've done it.

BOB

Oh dear!

FRANK (*starting to laugh*)

Thank God there wasn't much left.

BOB (*also laughing*)

I wish you could have seen your face when it went!

FRANK

Quiet a minute—listen!
(*There is the sound of footsteps on the stairs.*)

BOB

Here—I'd better 'op it.

148

FRANK

That's right, leave your best pal to face the barrage alone.

BOB

Come on, pull yourself together—we're for it.

FRANK

Chest up—chin up!
(*They are standing rigidly at attention when* ETHEL *comes into the room. She is wearing a dressing gown and her hair is in curlers.*)

ETHEL

And what d'you think you're doing, if I may make so bold?

FRANK

Bob was just going home.

ETHEL

Oh! Just going home, was he?

BOB

Sorry we woke you up, Ethel.

ETHEL

What was that you broke?

FRANK

Only the poor old Johnnie Walker.

ETHEL

I suppose you know what the time is, don't you?

FRANK

Who cares? Time was meant for slaves!

149

ETHEL

You go up to bed, Frank Gibbons. I'll have something to say to you later.

BOB

It was my fault, Ethel——

ETHEL

You ought to be ashamed of yourselves, both of you—men of your age—coming home drunk and waking up the whole house.

FRANK

You're not a whole house, Ethel, old girl—you're just—just a little bungalow—for better or for worse—— (*He giggles.*)

ETHEL

I'll give you bungalow! Go on, Bob, it's time you went home.

FRANK

Don't be hard on him, Ethel—he's my pal—he may be looking a bit silly now, I'll admit, but he's my pal all the same.

BOB

Who's looking silly?

FRANK

You do!

BOB

What about you?

ETHEL

You both look silly—but it's nothing to what you're going to look in the morning. Go on, Bob. I'm not going to stand here much longer catching me death.

150

BOB

All right—I can take a hint. Good night, Mrs. G. Good night, Sergeant. It's been a pleasure. (*To* FRANK.) Steady the Buffs!

(BOB *goes cheerfully, if a trifle unsteadily, out of the french window.* ETHEL *follows him up and locks it after him. She turns and regards* FRANK *thoughtfully for a moment.*)

FRANK (*holding up his hand*)

All right, all right—you don't have to say nothing! I know.

ETHEL

The next time you go to a regimental dinner you can go to a hotel afterwards and sleep it off. I won't have it, d'you hear? This is my dining-room, this is, not a bar parlour! Go on, get up to bed and don't make a noise either—— (*She turns and catches sight of* QUEENIE's *note on the mantelpiece.*) What's that?

FRANK

What's what?

ETHEL (*going to it*)

This letter.

FRANK

I haven't written no letters.

ETHEL (*taking it*)

It's Queenie's writing—— (*She opens it.*)

FRANK

Here—you can't read the girl's private letters.

151

ETHEL (*grimly*)

It's addressed to you and me.

FRANK

Well, I'll be damned!
  (ETHEL *reads the letter through and then stands quite still.* FRANK *goes over to her. She hands it to him.*)

ETHEL

She's gone. Read it. (*Sits down quietly in the chair by the fire and buries her face in her hands.*)

FRANK (*reads the letter carefully*)

Who's this man? Have you ever seen him?

ETHEL

No.

FRANK

I'll fetch her back—I'll give her the hiding of her life.

ETHEL

You can't find her. She doesn't say where she's gone.

FRANK (*reading*)

"—we love each other—his wife won't divorce him—we can't live without each other, so we are going away." (*He crumples the letter in his hand.*) It's our own fault—we might have known something like this would happen—we let her have her own way too much ever since she was a child— Queenie—— (*His voice breaks.*)
  (ETHEL *sits quite still without saying anything.*)
(*Kneeling on the floor by her chair.*): We'll trace her all right—don't you worry. We can find out who the man is

152

through the shop. It must have been there she met him.
We'll get her back.

ETHEL (*with sudden violence*)
I don't want her back! She's no child of mine. I don't want
ever to see her again as long as I live.

FRANK
Don't say that, Ethel.

ETHEL (*controlling herself*)
I mean it. I've done my best to bring her up to behave
respectable, to be a good girl, but it hasn't been any use.

FRANK
If she loves this man all that much—maybe it was too
strong for her—maybe she couldn't help herself——

ETHEL (*looking at him*)
You don't see what she's done the same way as I do—do
you?

FRANK
I don't know.

ETHEL
You and me never have quite seen eye to eye about what's
right and what's wrong. You'd have her back tomorrow
if she'd come, wouldn't you? But I wouldn't. You've always
encouraged her and told her how clever she was and let
her twist you round her little finger——

FRANK
All I've done is to try laughing at her instead of scolding
her.

153

ETHEL

Well, you've got something to laugh at now, haven't you?

FRANK

Don't go for me, Ethel—she's my girl as well as yours.

ETHEL

I'm not going for anybody. I've done my best. I can't do more.

FRANK

You can't stop loving the girl all at once, even if she has done wrong.

ETHEL

I can try.

FRANK

What's the sense of that?

ETHEL

It isn't anything to do with sense—it's how you feel.

FRANK

I've never seen you like this before—hard as nails you are.

ETHEL

What d'you expect me to be?

FRANK

I don't know—I suppose you never cared for Queenie as much as you did the other two.

ETHEL

It's not fair to say that.

154

FRANK

It's true though, isn't it?

ETHEL

No, it is not. She's almost been the most trouble, that's true enough, and she's certainly never put herself out to try and help me like Vi has; that's true, too, but I've cared for her just as much as the others, and don't you start saying I haven't. It's no use trying to lay the blame for this at my door. What she's done she's done on her own, and I'll never forgive her for it until the end of my days.

FRANK

If you feel like that it's not much good talking about it, is it? (*He gets up and walks away from her.*)

ETHEL (*after a pause—rising*)

Will you turn out or shall I?

FRANK (*turning pleadingly*)

Ethel——

ETHEL (*stonily*)

I'm going back to bed now. You might put those things back in the sideboard before you come up.

(*She goes out without looking at him. When she has gone he puts* QUEENIE's *letter in his pocket, goes wearily over to the table, and puts the biscuits, A1 Sauce, and bloater paste into the cupboard. He sits down at the table for a minute and finally buries his head in his arms as*

THE LIGHTS FADE.)

SCENE III

May, 1932. It is about four-thirty on a fine afternoon.

SCENE

The french windows are wide open. Out of sight in the garden FRANK *is weeding. From next door comes the sound of* BOB *mowing his lawn.*
MRS. FLINT *is knitting in her chair by the fireplace.* SYLVIA *is at the table with a newspaper and a dictionary, doing a crossword puzzle. A brand-new shining radio stands on a little table above the fireplace. It is playing softly.* EDIE *comes in and out with the tea-things.*

SYLVIA (*with satisfaction, scribbling*)
Got it!

MRS. F.
What?

SYLVIA
A biblical name in five letters with an *s* in the middle—Moses.

MRS. F.
I could have thought of that.

157

SYLVIA

Pity you didn't then; I asked you just now.

MRS. F.

Why's tea being laid so early?

SYLVIA

Because Frank's taking us to the Majestic.

MRS. F.

I wish somebody'd turn that wireless off—it's getting on my nerves.

SYLVIA (*rising*)

Ethel'd have it playing all day just because Reg gave it to her. (*She turns the radio off.*)

MRS. F.

Well, the skies'll fall next, I shouldn't wonder, you doing something I asked you without grumbling.

SYLVIA

Now then, Mrs. Flint, don't start.

MRS. F.

I wasn't starting anything, just passing a remark.

SYLVIA (*folding up the paper*)

Well, I've done that now, all except the long one across and the short one down with an *x* in it.

MRS. F.

I must say, having a steady job at the library's done you a world of good.

SYLVIA

I don't know what you're talking about.

MRS. F.

You're not so touchy as you used to be—flying off at the least thing.

SYLVIA (*primly*)

I'm very glad, I'm sure.

MRS. F.

It was a lucky day for all of us when you met that Mrs. Wilmot.

SYLVIA

I don't know to what you're referring.

MRS. F.

Oh yes, you do.

SYLVIA

I wish you'd stop going at me about everything for once.

MRS. F.

I was only saying it was a good thing, you meeting that Mrs. Wilmot.

SYLVIA

Well, we won't argue about it, will we?

MRS. F.

You haven't had one of your headaches for weeks, have you?

SYLVIA (*sharply*)

No, I have not.

MRS. F.

There you are, then.

SYLVIA

Perhaps you'd rather have me the way I was before—not sleeping a wink at night and suffering and being in error.

MRS. F.

In what?

SYLVIA

Error!

MRS. F.

Oh, so that's what it was.

SYLVIA

And you needn't sneer at Mrs. Wilmot either—she's a wonderful woman.

MRS. F.

She must be, to make you believe there wasn't anything the matter with you. It's what I've been saying for years.

SYLVIA (*brightly*)

Well, then, we won't say anything more about it, will we?

MRS. F.

We will if we feel like it.

(FRANK *comes in from the garden. He is in his shirt sleeves.*)

FRANK

How long before tea's ready?

EDIE (*on her way in with the milk and sugar*)

About five minutes—the kettle's on.

160

FRANK

Tell Ethel to start without me, Sylvia—I've got one more bed to do. Where is she?

SYLVIA

Upstairs lying down.

FRANK (*catching sight of a vase on the mantelpiece*)

Who put that May in here?

SYLVIA

I did—it's such a pretty colour.

FRANK (*taking it out of the vase*)

You ought to know better than to bring May into the house.

SYLVIA

Why ever not?

FRANK

It's unlucky.

SYLVIA (*with a great display of amusement*)

Why, Frank, really! What a thing to believe——

FRANK

You was born in the country the same as I was, Sylvia— it's a long while ago, I'll admit, but still——

SYLVIA (*tossing her head*)

There's no need to be nasty—you and your old May——

FRANK (*going out again*)

Well, don't do it again.

SYLVIA

Frank's been a changed man since Queenie went.

161

MRS. F.

I haven't noticed much difference.

SYLVIA

Do you think she'll ever come back?

MRS. F.

She'll get a piece of my mind if she does. Bringing disgrace on all of us.

SYLVIA

Frank had a letter from her the other day.

MRS. F.

How d'you know?

SYLVIA

It came by the midday post along with that letter I had from Mrs. Wilmot. Edie was upstairs doing the front room and I took it in myself. I recognised the handwriting——

MRS. F.

Think he told Ethel?

SYLVIA

Not very likely—she doesn't let him mention her name if she can help it. It had a French stamp.

MRS. F.

Disgusting!

ETHEL (*coming in*)

What's disgusting?

MRS. F.

Gracious, Ethel, what a start you gave me!

162

ETHEL
What was disgusting?

SYLVIA
A French stamp.

ETHEL
French stamp? What are you talking about?

SYLVIA
We were talking about the letter Frank had from Queenie.

ETHEL (*going over to the table*)
Oh, were you?

MRS. F.
Then it *was* from Queenie?

SYLVIA
You knew about it?

ETHEL
It's a pity that Christian Science of yours hasn't taught you to mind your own business among other things, Sylvia.

SYLVIA
Well, I'm sure I don't see what I've done!

ETHEL
You know perfectly well I won't 'ave Queenie's name spoken in this house. She's gone her own way, and that's that. She doesn't belong here any more.

MRS. F. (*with relish*)
I always knew that girl would come to no good.

163

ETHEL

Once and for all, will you hold your tongue, Mother! I'm sick to death of you and Sylvia gabbing and whispering behind my back.

MRS. F.

Well, I like that, I must say——

ETHEL

I don't care whether you like it or not—be quiet. Where's Frank?

SYLVIA (*sullenly*)

In the garden—he's started on another bed.

ETHEL

Tea's just ready.

SYLVIA

He said to begin without him.

(EDIE *comes in with the teapot.* ETHEL *sits down at the table and begins to pour out. There is a silence.* EDIE *goes out again.*)

SYLVIA (*to* MRS. FLINT)

Are you coming to the table or shall I bring it over to you?

MRS. F.

I'll stay here—the less I open my mouth, the better.

ETHEL

Here, Syl, take it over to her.

SYLVIA (*brings a cup of tea over to* MRS. F.)

Bread and butter?

MRS. F.

No, thank you. (*As* SYLVIA *turns to go*) I'll 'ave a petit beurre if there is one.

SYLVIA (*fetching her the plate of biscuits*)
All right.
(SYLVIA, *after* MRS. FLINT *has helped herself to biscuits, returns to the table and sits down. There is another silence.* ETHEL *gets up and turns on the radio again.*)

ETHEL

Sorry I flew out at you like that, Sylvia.

SYLVIA (*gracefully*)
It doesn't matter, I'm sure.

ETHEL

I dropped off to sleep on my bed this afternoon and had a bad dream.

SYLVIA

What was it?

ETHEL

I can't remember—I woke up feeling as if the world had come to an end.

SYLVIA (*cheerfully*)
Well, they say dreams go by contraries.

ETHEL

Yes, they do, don't they?

MRS. F.

These teeth of mine are getting worse and worse—I can't bite a thing.

165

ETHEL

Try soaking 'em.

MRS. F.

I am.

ETHEL

I wish Frank'd come in to his tea—we shall be late next thing we know.

SYLVIA

Why not take a cup out to him? He never eats much anyhow.

ETHEL (*glancing at the clock*)
It's nearly half-past now.

SYLVIA

I'll take it if you like.

ETHEL

No, I will. Once he starts weeding, he'd go on all night if we let him.
(ETHEL *pours out a cup of tea and goes out into the garden with it.*)

SYLVIA

You'd better be going upstairs to put your hat on, hadn't you?

MRS. F.

Lots of time. Frank'll have to wash before he goes.
(*There is a ring at the front doorbell.*)

SYLVIA

Now I wonder who that is?

166

MRS. F.

It might be Reg and Phyl.

SYLVIA

Can't be—they've gone to Sevenoaks with them friends of theirs.

MRS. F. (*listening*)

Has Edie gone?

SYLVIA

Yes—I heard her come out of the kitchen.
(*The door opens and* VI *comes quickly into the room. She looks pale and is trembling.*)
Why, Vi, whatever's the matter?

VI

Where are Mum and Dad?

SYLVIA

In the garden.

VI (*hurriedly*

Take Granny upstairs—there's been an accident—it's Reg and Phyl—I've got to tell Mum and Dad.

MRS. F.

What's that?

SYLVIA

What sort of an accident? What happened?

VI

They were in Reg's car and a lorry came out of a turning——

167

SYLVIA
Are they badly hurt?

VI
They're dead.

SYLVIA
Oh, my God!

VI
Mrs. Goulding was with them; she knew I had a telephone
and so she rung me up from the hospital. She was in the
back and got thrown out. Please take Granny upstairs—I
must tell them alone.

SYLVIA (*bursting into tears*)
Oh, my God! Oh, my God!

VI
Don't cry, Auntie Sylvia—they'll hear you—don't let them
hear you.

SYLVIA (*sobbing*)
I can't believe it—I can't——

MRS. F.
Help me up.

VI (*doing so*)
Auntie Sylvia—please——

(SYLVIA, *with a great effort at control but still sobbing,*
helps MRS. FLINT *out of the room.*
VI *closes her eyes for a minute, braces herself, and goes*
out into the garden. The room is empty for a minute or
two, and there is no sound except the radio playing

168

softly and the mowing machine next door. Presently FRANK *and* ETHEL *come in alone. His arm is round her and they neither of them speak. He brings her slowly to the chair by the fireplace and puts her gently down into it. Then he draws up another chair and sits next to her. He reaches out for her hand and they sit there in silence as*

THE LIGHTS FADE.)

ACT THREE

SCENE I

TIME
December 10, 1936.

SCENE
It is just after ten o'clock in the evening. The remains of supper have been pushed aside to make way for the radio, which is standing in the middle of the table.
Round it are sitting FRANK, ETHEL, SYLVIA, VI, *and* SAM.
King Edward VIII's farewell broadcast after his abdication is just finishing. SYLVIA *is in tears. Everyone else is silent.*
FRANK *and* ETHEL *have aged a good deal in the four years since* REG'S *death. They are only fifty-two and fifty-one respectively, nevertheless they look older.* SYLVIA, *on the other hand, who is after all the same age as* ETHEL, *looks, if anything, a little younger than before. This is doubtless attributable to the assurance acquired from Christian Science and the brisk example of Mrs. Wilmot.* VI *and* SAM *appear to be the settled, comfortable married couple that they are.* SAM *indeed, having put on weight, seems definitely middle-aged.*
At the end of the broadcast the radio makes a few discordant wheezes and groans. FRANK *gets up and turns it off.*

173

FRANK

Well—that's that. (*He gets himself a cigarette from the mantelpiece.*) There won't be anything more to listen to to-night, all the stations have closed down.

SYLVIA (*sobbing*)

It's dreadful—dreadful——

FRANK

Anyway, it's no use going on about it now.

SYLVIA

It was a wonderful speech—fairly broke your heart to listen to it. (*She blows her nose.*)

FRANK

Well—I suppose he had to make it, but I somehow wish he hadn't.

(*There is silence for a moment, broken only by* SYLVIA'S *sniffs.* ETHEL *gets up and takes a calendar down from the wall by the fireplace.*)

SYLVIA

Ethel—what are you doing?

ETHEL (*going out of the room with it*)

It's near the end of the year anyhow.

VI (*getting up*)

Better put the radio back where it belongs. Give me a hand, Sam.

(*They move the radio back onto its little table.*)

SAM

We'll have to be going in a minute. Mrs. Burgess said she couldn't stay after half-past ten and we can't leave the children in the house all by themselves.

174

VI

I'll pop up and get me hat—I left it in Mum's room. (*She goes out.*)

SAM

How's the library going, Aunt Sylvia?

SYLVIA (*putting the table straight*)
All right—but I'm leaving it next month.

SAM

I thought you liked working there.

SYLVIA

Oh, it's not bad, but I'm going in with Mrs. Wilmot. She wants me to assist her in her reading and rest room in Baker Street.

SAM
Oh, I see.

SYLVIA
How are the children?

SAM

Sheila's all right, but Joan's been a bit seedy the last few days.

SYLVIA (*brightly*)
Poor little thing.

SAM

The doctor said she never quite got over that cold she had in November.

SYLVIA (*indulgently*)
Did he indeed?

175

SAM (*slightly nettled*)

Yes, he did. She was running a bit of a temperature a couple of nights ago, so we've kept her in bed ever since.

SYLVIA

I suppose if you believe in doctors, it's best to do what they say.

SAM

Well, it stands to reason they know a bit more about it than we do, doesn't it?

SYLVIA

No, I don't think it does! (*She lightly hums a little tune.*)

SAM (*incensed*)

What would you do if you broke your leg? I suppose you'd send for a doctor then, wouldn't you?

SYLVIA (*putting some things into the sideboard cupboard*)

I wouldn't break my leg.

SAM (*pressing*)

But if you *did*? If you were run over through no fault of your own——

SYLVIA

I should certainly send for treatment.

SAM

There you are then!

SYLVIA (*with a pitying smile*)

You don't understand, Sam. After all, there isn't any reason why you should. You haven't studied the matter, have you?

176

SAM

No, I haven't.

SYLVIA

It wouldn't be surgical treatment I should send for. It would be spiritual treatment.

SAM

Would that heal a compound fracture?

SYLVIA

Certainly.

SAM

Before I'd believe that I'd have to see it with my own eyes.

SYLVIA

If you believed first, you wouldn't have to worry whether you saw it with your own eyes or not.

SAM

Oh yes, I should.

SYLVIA (*with sweet, unassailable superiority*)

Dear Sam!
    (FRANK *comes back.*)

FRANK

Where's Ethel?

SYLVIA

In the kitchen, I think.

FRANK

We miss Edie and that's a fact. I've tried to make her get someone else, but she won't.

177

SYLVIA

There's not so much to do since Mrs. Flint passed on.

FRANK

I do wish you wouldn't talk like that, Sylvia, it sounds so soft.

SYLVIA

I don't know what you mean, I'm sure.

FRANK (*firmly*)

Mother died, see! First of all she got flu and that turned to pneumonia and the strain of that affected her heart, which was none too strong at the best of times, and she DIED. Nothing to do with passing on at all.

SYLVIA

How do you know?

FRANK

I admit it's only your new way of talking, but it gets me down, see?

(ETHEL *comes in again, followed by* VI *in her hat and coat.*)

ETHEL

What are you shouting about?

FRANK

I'm not shouting about anything at all. I'm merely explaining to Sylvia that Mother died. She didn't pass on or pass over or pass out—she DIED.

VI (*giggling*)

Oh, Dad, you do make me laugh, really you do!

178

ETHEL

It's not a fit subject to talk about anyhow.

VI

Come on, Sam—we must be going. Good night, Mother.

ETHEL

Good night, dear. If you want to go out tomorrow afternoon I'll come and look after the children.

VI

Thanks a lot. Good night, Dad.

FRANK (*kissing her*)

So long, Vi.

VI

Good night, Auntie Sylvia. Don't pay any attention to Dad. He's an old tease.

SAM

Good night, all.

FRANK

I'll come to the door with you. Where's Archie—Ethel?

ETHEL

Asleep in the kitchen. He's been out once tonight.

FRANK (*escorting* VI *and* SAM *out*)

I'll tell you one thing. As a mouser, Archie knocks poor old Percy into a cocked hat!

(*They go out.*)

SYLVIA

I think I'll go up to bed now, Ethel.

179

ETHEL

All right, dear.

SYLVIA

What about the washing up?

ETHEL

I'll do the lot tomorrow morning. I've left everything in the sink for tonight.

SYLVIA (*dutifully kissing her*)
Then good night.

ETHEL

Good night.

SYLVIA (*sighing as she goes out*)
Oh dear!
(ETHEL *glances at the clock and then, taking some socks out of a workbasket on the table by the fireplace, sits down in the armchair and begins to darn.* FRANK *comes back.*)

FRANK

Vi's looking a bit peaky, isn't she?

ETHEL

She's worried about Joan, I think.

FRANK

She'll be all right. Remember the trouble we had with Queenie when she was tiny?

ETHEL (*coldly*)
Yes, I do.

180

FRANK
Sorry—I forgot.

ETHEL
You're lucky.

FRANK (*sadly*)
You are a funny woman, Ethel, and no mistake.

ETHEL
I expect I am. We're as God made us, I suppose, and there's nothing to be done about it.

FRANK
Well, all I can say is He might have done a better job on some people without straining Himself.

ETHEL
How often have I told you I won't 'ave you talking like that, Frank?

FRANK
I wasn't meaning you.

ETHEL
I don't care who you was meaning. If you don't believe in anything yourself, you can at least have the decency to spare the feelings of them as do.

FRANK
As a matter of fact, I believe in a whole lot of things.

ETHEL
Well, that's nice to know.

181

FRANK

One of 'em is that being bitter about anybody isn't a good thing, let alone if it happens to be your own daughter.

ETHEL

I'm not bitter. I just don't think of her any more, that's all.

FRANK

That's one of the things I don't believe.

ETHEL

Don't let's talk about it, shall we?

FRANK

I wish you'd have another girl in place of Edie.

ETHEL

I don't need one now there's only the three of us. Sylvia helps every now and again and the char does the heavy cleaning once a week.

FRANK

We could afford it quite easily.

ETHEL

Maybe we could—but getting a strange girl used to our ways would be more trouble than it was worth.

FRANK

What anybody ever wanted to marry Edie for beats me.

ETHEL

No reason why they shouldn't. She was a good girl and a good worker.

FRANK

Exactly the reasons I married you.

182

ETHEL

Don't talk so silly.

FRANK

She may not be much to look at—I said to myself—but there's a worker if ever I saw one!

ETHEL

Haven't you got anything better to do than to sit there making funny remarks?

FRANK

There's nothing much I want to do.

ETHEL

Why don't you have a nice read of the paper?

FRANK

There's nothing in it but the abdication, and I'm fed up with that.

(*There is a tap on the window.*)

ETHEL

That'll be Bob. Now I can get on with me darning.

(**FRANK** *goes to the window, opens it, and admits* **BILLY.** **BILLY** *is now thirty-one and wearing the uniform of a Warrant Officer. He has grown a little more solid with the years, but apart from this there is not much change in him.*)

FRANK

Well, here's a surprise!

BILLY

Hallo, Mr. Gibbons.

183

ETHEL

Why, Billy—I'd no idea you was back.

BILLY (*shaking hands with her*)

I've been transferred from a cruiser to a destroyer—I've got a couple of weeks' leave.

FRANK

D'you like that?

BILLY

You bet I do.

FRANK

What's the difference?

BILLY

Oh, lots of little things. To start with, I live in the ward-room—then I keep watches when we're at sea—and, well, it's sort of more friendly, if you know what I mean.

FRANK

Like a drink?

BILLY

No, thanks. I just had one with Dad.

ETHEL

Is he coming in?

BILLY

Yes, I think so—a bit later on.

ETHEL

He must be glad you're back. It must be lonely for him in that house all by himself since your mother was taken.

184

FRANK

Nora DIED, Ethel! Nobody took her.

ETHEL

You ought to be ashamed, talking like that in front of Billy.

BILLY

It was a blessed release, really, you know, Mrs. Gibbons, what with one thing and another. She'd been bedridden so long——

FRANK

Hear the speech?

BILLY

Yes.

FRANK

What did you think of it?

BILLY

Oh, I don't know—a bit depressing—taken all round. He was popular in the Service, you know.

FRANK

Yes—I expect he was.

BILLY

He came on board a ship I was in once, in the Mediterranean; that was about five years ago, when I was still a T.G.M.

ETHEL

What's that?

BILLY

Torpedo Gunner's Mate.

185

FRANK

All them initials in the Navy. I can't think how you remember 'em.

BILLY

Oh, you get used to it.

ETHEL

Would you like me to go and make you a cup of tea? It won't take a minute.

BILLY

No, thanks, Mrs. Gibbons—there's something I want to talk to you about as a matter of fact—both of you.

FRANK

All right, son—what is it?

BILLY (*nervously*)

Got a cigarette on you? I left mine next door.

FRANK (*producing a packet*)

Here you are.

BILLY (*taking one*)

Thanks.

FRANK

Match?

BILLY (*striking one of his own*)

Got one, thanks.

FRANK (*after a slight pause*)

Well?

186

BILLY

I feel a bit awkward, really—I wanted Dad to come with me and back me up, but he wouldn't.

FRANK

A man of your age hanging onto his father's coattails? I never 'eard of such a thing. What have you been up to?

ETHEL (*with sudden premonition, sharply*)
What is it, Billy?

BILLY

It's about Queenie.
(*There is silence for a moment.*)

ETHEL (*hardening*)
What about her?

BILLY

Does it still make you angry—even to hear her name?

ETHEL

I'm not angry.

FRANK

Have you seen her, Billy?

BILLY

Yes—I've seen her.

FRANK (*eagerly*)
How is she?

BILLY

Fine.
(*There is another silence. BILLY mooches about the room a bit.*)

187

ETHEL (*with an obvious effort*)
What is it that you wanted to say about Queenie, Billy?

BILLY (*in a rush*)
I sympathise with how you feel, Mrs. Gibbons—really I do
—and what's more, she does too. She knows what a wrong
she did you in going off like that. It didn't take her long to
realise it. She hasn't had any too good a time, you know. In
fact, she's been through a good deal. He left her—the man
she went off with—Major Blount—after about a year. He
went back to his wife. He left Queenie stranded in a sort of
boardinghouse in Brussels.

ETHEL (*bitterly*)
How soon was it before she found another man to take her
on?

FRANK
Ethel!

BILLY
A long time—over three years.

ETHEL (*bending over her darning*)
She's all right now then, isn't she?

BILLY
Yes—she's all right now.

FRANK
What sort of a bad time did she have? How d'you mean?

BILLY
Trying to earn a living for herself—getting in and out of
different jobs. She showed dresses off in a dressmaker's shop
for over a year, I believe, but the shop went broke, and then
she got herself a place to look after some English children.

It wasn't a very long job. She just had to take them across France to Marseilles and put them on a ship to go out to their parents in India. By that time she had a little money saved and was coming home to England to try and get her old manicuring job back when she got ill with appendicitis and was taken to hospital——

FRANK

Where—where was she taken to hospital? How long ago?

BILLY

Paris—about a year ago. Then, when she was in the hospital, she picked up with an old Scotswoman who was in the next bed, and a little while later the two of them started an old English tearoom in Menton in the South of France—you know, just for the English visitors—that's where I ran into her by accident. We were doing a summer cruise and the ship I was in laid off a place called Villefranche for a few days. A couple of pals and I hired a taxi to go for a drive and stopped at Menton to have a cup of tea—and there she was!

ETHEL

Is she there now?

BILLY

No, she isn't there now.

FRANK

Where is she then?

BILLY

She's here.

ETHEL

Here!

189

FRANK

How d'you mean—here?

BILLY

Next door with Dad.

ETHEL (*jumping to her feet and dropping her darning on the floor*)

Billy!

BILLY

We were married last week in a registry office in Plymouth.

ETHEL

Married!

BILLY (*simply*)

I've always loved her, you know—I always said I'd wait for her.

FRANK (*brokenly*)

Oh, son—I can't believe it. Oh, son!

(*He wrings* BILLY's *hand wildly and then almost runs out through the french windows.*)

BILLY

You'll forgive her now, won't you, Mrs. Gibbons?

ETHEL (*in a strained voice*)

I don't seem to have any choice, do I?

BILLY

I always thought you'd like to have me for a son——

ETHEL

Better late than never—that's what it is, isn't it? (*She starts half laughing and crying at the same time.*) Better late than —never—oh dear!——

(*He takes her in his arms and after holding her close for a moment places her gently in the chair.*)

BILLY

Shall I get you a little nip of something?

ETHEL (*tearfully*)

Yes, please——

BILLY

Where is it?

ETHEL

In the sideboard cupboard.

(BILLY *goes quickly to the sideboard, opens the cupboard, takes a bottle of whisky out, and pours some, neat, into a glass. He brings it to her. He gives her the glass and she sips a little. He takes her left hand and pats it affectionately.* FRANK *comes back through the window leading* QUEENIE *by the hand. She is soberly dressed and looks pale. There is a strained silence for a moment.*)

QUEENIE

Hallo, Mum.

ETHEL

So you've come back, have you—you bad girl.

QUEENIE (*coming slowly across the room to her*)

Yes, Mum.

ETHEL (*putting her arms round her*)

A nice way to behave, I must say—upsetting me like this——

THE LIGHTS FADE.

SCENE II

September 30, 1938.

SCENE
It is about nine o'clock in the evening.
ETHEL *and* QUEENIE *have finished their supper and gone upstairs to see if* QUEENIE's *four months' old son is sleeping all
right.* SYLVIA *and* VI *are still at the table.*

SYLVIA
Is there any more hot water in the jug?

VI
No—there isn't.

SYLVIA
I thought I'd like another cup.

VI (*jumping up*)
I'll run and get some.

SYLVIA (*not moving*)
Don't worry, dear—I'll go.

VI
You stay where you are, Auntie Syl—it won't take a minute.
(*She runs out with the jug.* SYLVIA, *left alone, sits pen-*

sively with her chin resting on her hands. In a moment or two VI *returns with the hot water.*)

SYLVIA (*as she comes in*)
I always knew it, you know.

VI
Always knew what?

SYLVIA
That there wouldn't be a war.

VI
Well, I thought there would, I must say, otherwise I shouldn't have sent Sheila and Joan down to Mrs. Marsh in Dorset.

SYLVIA
I know you did, dear. Your mother was worried, too, about Queenie and little Frankie—but I wasn't. Neither was Mrs. Wilmot.

VI
Fancy that now.

SYLVIA
Mrs. Wilmot laughed outright, you know, when the woman came to try on her gas mask. "Take that stupid thing away," she said. Just like that—quite simply. The woman was furious.

VI
I'm not surprised.

SYLVIA
It's funny how cross people get when you refuse to believe in evil.

194

VI

It's rather difficult not to believe in evil, Auntie Syl, when you think of what's going on in differents parts of the world just now.

SYLVIA

If enough people believed in good, none of it would happen.

VI

Yes, but they don't, do they?

SYLVIA

You remind me of your father sometimes, Vi; you're material-minded.

VI

Well, I can't help that, can I?

SYLVIA

Well, if you don't mind me saying so—I think you can.

VI

As far as I can see, facts are facts, Auntie Syl, and if looking at it like that means I'm material-minded I'm afraid that's what I shall go on being.

SYLVIA

You don't understand what I mean, dear.

VI

No—I'm afraid I don't.

SYLVIA

To begin with, what you call facts may not be facts at all.

VI

What are they then?

195

SYLVIA

Illusion—and error.

VI

Isn't error a fact then?

SYLVIA (*a little nettled*)

Of course it is in a way—that's just the trouble. But still if you admit it's a fact and regard it as a fact, it makes it more of a fact than ever, doesn't it?

VI

I shouldn't think it made much difference one way or the other.

SYLVIA

But it DOES!

VI

You mean that when Sheila had toothache the other day I ought to have told her that she hadn't.

SYLVIA

I don't mean any such thing.

VI

What do you mean then?

SYLVIA

I mean that if she had been brought up to believe that pain is evil and that evil doesn't really exist at all, she wouldn't have had toothache in the first place.

VI

But she'd broken it on a bit of toffee and the nerve was exposed.

SYLVIA
Nonsense.

VI
It isn't nonsense, Auntie Syl, it's true.

SYLVIA
I wish Mrs. Wilmot was here.

VI
I'm sure I'm glad she isn't.

SYLVIA
It shows a very small mind to talk like that, Vi—you ought to be ashamed. Mrs. Wilmot is a very remarkable woman.

VI
She sounds a bit silly to me.

SYLVIA
We will not discuss the matter any further.

VI
All right.

SYLVIA
Your very life has been saved at this moment by the triumph of right thinking over wrong thinking.

VI (*equably*)
Well, that's nice, isn't it?

SYLVIA
I've often thought Mr. Chamberlain must be a Christian Scientist at heart.

197

VI

Well, let's hope that Hitler and Mussolini are too, and then we shall all be on velvet.

(FRANK *comes in, his hat and coat on.*)

FRANK

What are you two looking so glum about?

VI

We were talking about Mr. Chamberlain; Auntie Syl says she thinks he must be a Christian Scientist.

FRANK (*going out again*)

That might account for a lot.

SYLVIA

What did you want to say that for, Vi? You're a very aggravating girl.

VI

Sorry.

SYLVIA

Just because you haven't any faith in anything yourself, you think it's funny to laugh at people who have.

VI

I wasn't laughing at all.

FRANK (*having taken off his hat and coat*)

Where's your mother?

VI

Upstairs with Queenie and his lordship.

198

FRANK

Nothing wrong with him, is there?

VI

Oh no—he's fine. Queenie's not feeling any too good, so she went to bed—her leg was hurting her a bit. It's nothing serious; the doctor came this afternoon to have a look at her and said it was only brought on by the strain of the last week——

FRANK

I'll go up in a minute.

SYLVIA

Did you see anything of the crowds?

FRANK (*laconically*)

Yes, I did.

VI

We heard him arrive at the airport, on the radio.

FRANK (*sitting down*)

So did I.

VI

Sam's meeting me at the Strand Corner House a little later on. We thought we'd have a look at the West End. It ought to be exciting.

FRANK

Well, it's exciting all right, if you like to see a lot of people yelling themselves hoarse without the faintest idea what they're yelling about.

199

SYLVIA

How can you, Frank! They're cheering because we've been saved from war.

FRANK

I'll cheer about that when it's proved to me.

SYLVIA (*hotly*)

You wouldn't care if there was another war. You're one of those people that think it doesn't matter that millions and millions of innocent people should be bombed! Just because you enjoyed yourself in the last one——

FRANK (*firmly*)

Now listen here, Sylvia. Don't you talk to me like that because I won't 'ave it—see? I did *not* enjoy myself in the last war—nobody but a bloody fool without any imagination would ever say that he did. And I do not think it doesn't matter if millions and millions of innocent people are bombed! So you can get them silly ideas out of your head to start with. But what I would like to say is this. I've seen something today that I wouldn't 'ave believed could happen in this country. I've seen thousands of people, English people, mark you, carrying on like maniacs, shouting and cheering with relief, for no other reason but that they'd been thoroughly frightened, and it made me sick and that's a fact! I only hope to God that we shall have guts enough to learn one lesson from this and that we shall never find ourselves in a position again when we have to appease anybody!

SYLVIA

All you men think about is having Guts and being Top Dog and killing each other, but I'm a woman and I don't care how much we appease as long as we don't have a war. War is wicked and evil and vile. They that live by the sword shall die by the sword. It's more blessed to give than to receive——

FRANK

I don't think it's more blessed to give in and receive a nice kick on the bottom for doing it.

ETHEL (*coming in*)

Will you two stop shouting—you'll wake up Frankie!

SYLVIA

He's a warmonger, that's all he is—a warmonger.

FRANK

Judging by the 'eavy way you're breathing, Sylvia, I should say you was in error!

SYLVIA (*bursting into tears of rage*)

You're no brother of mine—I don't want to speak to you ever again——

(*She rushes out of the room and slams the door.*)

ETHEL

What's the use of arguing with her, Frank? You know it never does any good.

VI

She started it, Mother. She was ever so silly. She's getting sillier and sillier every day.

ETHEL

Don't you talk about your aunt Sylvia like that.

VI (*kissing her*)

Dear old Mum, I'm thirty-three, you know, now, not fifteen.

ETHEL

All the more reason for you to know better.

VI

There you are, you see! Mum'll never learn.

ETHEL

I don't care if you're a hundred and five, I won't have you being saucy to your aunt Sylvia, or to me either, for that matter.

VI

What about Dad? I can be saucy to him, can't I?

ETHEL

Get on with you, Miss Sharp!

VI

I'm just going anyhow—I'm picking up Sam—we're going to see the crowds. (*She laughs at* FRANK.) Sorry, Dad——

FRANK

You can cheer your head off, for all I care.

VI

Maybe I will—I'll just pop up and see Queenie for a minute. Good night, all. . . .

FRANK

Good night.

ETHEL

Don't forget to send round that pram.

202

VI

Sam'll bring it tomorrow. (*She goes out.*)

ETHEL (*sitting down*)
What a week! I wouldn't have believed I could be so tired.

FRANK
Yes—you look a bit done up. How's Queenie?

ETHEL
She's all right. You'd think nobody'd ever had a baby before! All the fuss we've had the last month.

FRANK
She got up too soon.

ETHEL
She had a letter from Billy this afternoon. He wants her to go out there.

FRANK
She can't yet, she's not strong enough.

ETHEL
He didn't say yet—he said after Christmas—all being well.

FRANK
The baby won't be old enough to travel.

ETHEL
She'll leave him here.

FRANK
With us?

ETHEL

Of course—don't be so silly—who else would she leave it
with! She won't be gone more than a year, anyway.

FRANK

That'll be fine, won't it?

ETHEL

Fine for you, maybe—you won't have to look after it.

FRANK

Perhaps you'd rather she left it with Vi! Or in a home of
some sort.

ETHEL

Don't be a bigger fool than you can help—go on upstairs
and say good night to her before she drops off.

FRANK

I'm expecting Bob to come in and have a farewell binge.
Give me a shout when he comes.

ETHEL

Binge, indeed! One small one's all you're going to have, my
lad, if I have to come down and take the bottle away from
you.

FRANK (*cheerfully—going out*)

I'd like to see you try.

(*Left alone,* ETHEL *gets up and goes over to the sideboard cupboard. She takes out the whisky bottle, a
syphon, and two glasses. She has just done this when*
BOB *taps at the window. She lets him in.*)

BOB

Hallo, Ethel.

ETHEL

Frank's just saying good night to Queenie—he'll be down in a minute.

BOB

What a week! What with the crisis and the sand bags and me having to pack up all the furniture into the bargain.

ETHEL

Has most of it gone?

BOB

Yes—went this afternoon. I'm sleeping on a camp bed to-night.

ETHEL

Frank'll miss you. So shall I.

BOB

I'm not going very far. You'll both come down and see me, won't you?

ETHEL

Of course we will, Bob. I've often wondered why you stayed on so long in that house all by yourself.

BOB

Oh, I don't know. It was near you and Frank—and it was somewhere for Billy to come home to.

ETHEL

You'll feel a bit lost, I expect—living in the country.

205

BOB

Well, I shall have me garden—a damn sight nicer one than I've got here—and there's the sea nearby—and the village pub!

ETHEL

We'll come down and see you quite soon. I'll go and tell Frank you're here.

BOB

Righto. (*There is a slight pause.*) Good-bye, Ethel.

ETHEL (*uncertainly*)

Good-bye, Bob. (*She goes to him and kisses him.*) Take care of yourself.
(*She goes swiftly out of the room. After a moment* FRANK *comes in.*)

FRANK

Well, he's back. Umbrella and all!

BOB

Yes.

FRANK

Let's have a drink. I'm feeling a bit low—what with one thing and another. (*He starts to pour out the drinks.*) Only one good thing's happened.

BOB

What's that?

FRANK

If Queenie goes out to Singapore after Christmas, we're taking charge of the kid.

206

BOB

I thought you'd get him.

FRANK

Well, you couldn't have had him—all alone by the sad sea waves.

BOB

All right, all right, no hard feelings.

FRANK (*holding up his glass*)

Here goes.

BOB (*doing the same*)

Happy days!

FRANK

Remember the first night we moved in? When we had Sylvia's Wincarnis?

BOB

That's going back a bit.

FRANK

Nearly twenty years.

BOB

And here we are—just the same.

FRANK

Are we?

BOB (*with a sigh*)

No—I suppose we're not.

FRANK

It's a strange world.

207

BOB

You've said it.

FRANK

All them years—all the things that happened in 'em—I wouldn't go back over them for all the rice in China—would you?

BOB

Not on your life.

FRANK

Remember that picnic we 'ad at Box Hill in 1923 and you got squiffy and fell down and sprained your ankle?

BOB

Whatever made you think of that?

FRANK

I don't know, I was just thinking——

BOB

Remember that summer holiday—the one we all had together—before Nora got ill?

FRANK

The year we went to Bognor?

BOB

That's right.

FRANK

That must have been earlier still. Let's see, Reg was fourteen—that would have been 1921. . . .

BOB

I remember you and Ethel having a row about going out in a boat.

FRANK

Yes. . . . (*He laughs.*) Ethel's always hated going out in a boat.

BOB

I remember the night we went to your regimental dinner too—the night Queenie went off. . . .

FRANK

Reg was still alive then, wasn't he?

BOB

Yes—that was about a year before.

FRANK (*looking round*)

I wonder what 'appens to rooms when people give 'em up —go away and leave the house empty.

BOB

How d'you mean?

FRANK

I don't know. I was just thinking about you going away from next door after all that time and me and Ethel going away, too, pretty soon. I shouldn't think we'd stay on here much longer—and wondering what the next people that live in this room will be like—whether they'll feel any bits of us left about the place. . . .

BOB

'Ere, shut up! You're giving me the willies!

209

FRANK

Have another spot?

BOB

Just a small one.

FRANK (*at sideboard*)

Funny you going to live just near where I was born.

BOB

It's about eleven miles, isn't it?

FRANK

Less than that if you go by the marsh road, but it takes longer. I'll probably come back there one day, I hope—that is, if I can get round Ethel. She hates the country.

BOB

I suppose it's all according to what you're used to.

FRANK (*handing him his drink*)

You don't think the Germans will ever get here, do you?

BOB

No—of course I don't.

FRANK

I'm feeling a bit bad about all this business.

BOB

I'm not feeling too good myself.

FRANK

I'm going to miss you a hell of a lot.

BOB

Same here. You'll be coming down though, won't you?

FRANK
You bet.

BOB (*lifting his glass*)
Happy days, old pal.

FRANK (*doing the same*)
Happy days, old pal!

THE LIGHTS FADE.

SCENE III

TIME
June, 1939.

SCENE
*It is a warm summer evening and the french windows are
wide open. It is still daylight and, as in Act One, Scene I,
the May tree is in bloom at the end of the garden. Also as in
Act One, Scene I, the room is almost empty of furniture.
The pictures have been taken down from the walls and curtains from the windows. There is a muddle of packing cases,
luggage, parcels, shavings, paper, and string. The mantelpiece is denuded of ornaments, but the armchair is still by
the fireplace, and the sideboard, looking strangely bare, is
still in its accustomed place, although jutting out from the
wall a trifle, as if it were afraid of being left behind. From
upstairs comes the sound of intermittent hammering.*
*VI comes in from the garden wheeling a pram. She wheels it
carefully through the window and brings it to a standstill
just above the armchair. She gives a look to see if its occu-
pant is all right, and then goes to the door.*

   VI (*calling*)
Mum . . .

   ETHEL (*off stage*)
Yes, dear?

VI

I'll have to be getting along now.

ETHEL

All right, dear.

VI

I've brought him in.

(ETHEL *appears. She looks a little flustered and untidy.*)

ETHEL

Has he been good?

VI

Good as gold. I gave him the post card Queenie sent with the camel on it—he liked it.

ETHEL (*looking into the pram*)

He's dropped off now.

VI

There's nothing more I can do to help, is there?

ETHEL

No, thanks, dear—everything's done now. They're coming for the rest of the stuff in the morning. I'm just getting a bit of supper for your dad and me in the kitchen—we're going to walk round to the flat afterwards.

VI

I do hope you'll like it, Mum.

ETHEL

Well, it's got a nice view of the Common, I will say that for it.

VI

You'll find it easier being on one floor, of course.

ETHEL

Yes—I suppose I will.

VI

It looked quite nice to me—a bit modernistic, of course.

ETHEL

Well, that can't be helped.

VI

It'll be a comfort, anyway, having running hot water instead of having to fuss about with a geyser.

ETHEL

One thing less for your dad to grumble about.

VI (*listening*)

He's enjoying himself with that hammer, isn't he?

ETHEL

The more noise the better's his motto.

VI (*calling*)

Dad . . .

FRANK (*upstairs*)

Hallo . . .

VI

I'm going now.

FRANK

Righto—see you in the morning.

VI

Good night, Mum.

ETHEL (*kissing her absently*)
Good night, dear.

VI

I'll bring Archie round tomorrow when I come. The children'll miss him.

ETHEL

I don't see why you don't keep him really, you know. After all, you've got a little garden, which is more than we'll have in the new flat.

VI

Oh, Mum—what'll Dad say?

ETHEL

He won't mind much. Poor old Percy was his choice, you know. He never took to Archie in the same way.

VI

Thanks ever so much, Mum. If you feel after a time you want him back all you've got to do is just say.

ETHEL

All right, dear.

VI

Well—so long.

ETHEL

Thank you for coming, dear—give my love to Sam and the children.

216

VI
I will. Good night.

ETHEL
Good night. . . .
(VI *goes out.* ETHEL *bustles about the room a little, then gives one more look into the pram and sits down in the armchair with a sigh of weariness.* FRANK *comes downstairs and into the room. He is in his shirt sleeves and carries a hammer.*)

FRANK
Hallo—having a breather?

ETHEL
I am that. My back's breaking.

FRANK (*putting the hammer down on the sideboard*)
Not as young as you were.

ETHEL
Who are you to talk?

FRANK
How's his lordship? (*He looks into the pram.*)

ETHEL
Don't wake him up now.

FRANK
He's dribbling—dirty boy.

ETHEL
I expect you dribbled when you were his age.

FRANK

I do still as a matter of fact, if I happen to drop off in the afternoon.

ETHEL

Well, it's nothing to boast about.

FRANK

Bit snappy, aren't we?

ETHEL

Who wouldn't be with all I've had to do today!

FRANK (*bending over her and giving her a kiss*)

Poor old crock.

ETHEL

Leave off, Frank—we haven't got time for fooling about.

FRANK

That's just where you're wrong. We've got all the time in the world.

ETHEL

All right—have it your own way.

FRANK (*sitting on a packing case*)

I shall miss that garden.

ETHEL

Well, it's your own fault—you're the one that wanted to move.

FRANK

I know.

218

ETHEL

You'll have the balcony anyhow. You can put window boxes all round it.

FRANK

One day—a bit later on—when I stop working, we might get a little place in the country, mightn't we?

ETHEL

And when will that be, may I ask?

FRANK

Oh, I don't know. In a few years, I suppose.

ETHEL

Well, we'll think about that when the time comes.

FRANK

I think you'd like the country, you know, Ethel, once you got used to it.

ETHEL

That's as may be.

FRANK

I know you're frightened of it being a bit too quiet for you, but when people get old they don't mind so much about being quiet.

ETHEL

We're not all that old yet, you know.

FRANK

We ought to go abroad someday, by rights.

ETHEL

Whatever for?

FRANK

Well, I feel a bit silly sometimes, having been over other people's journeys for twenty years and never so much as set foot out of England myself since 1919.

ETHEL

Well, if you want to go gadding about to foreign parts you'll have to do it by yourself.

FRANK

What a chance! You'd be after me like an electric hare.

ETHEL

You flatter yourself.

FRANK (*pensively*)

It's a funny thing . . .

ETHEL

What is?

FRANK

You'd think taking all the furniture out of a room would make it look bigger, but this one looks smaller.

ETHEL (*with a touch of vehemence*)

I shall be glad when we're out of it.

FRANK

So shall I—sorry, too, though, in a way.

ETHEL (*rising*)

Well, I've rested long enough—I must go and get on with the supper. . . .

(FRANK *gets up, too, and quite quietly puts his arm round her. She submits and rests her head on his shoulder. They stand there together in silence for a moment.*)

FRANK

It's been a long time all right.

ETHEL

Yes.

FRANK (*gently*)

I don't mind how many flats we move into or where we go or what we do, as long as I've got you. . . .

ETHEL (*in a low voice*)

Don't talk so silly. . . .

> (*She disentangles herself from his arms and goes quickly out of the room with her head down.* FRANK *looks after her for a moment, smiling, then he takes a packet of cigarettes from his pocket, lights one, and saunters over to the pram. He stands looking down into it for a little.*)

FRANK

Hallo, cock! So you've decided to wake up, 'ave you? Feel like a bit of upsie-downsie? (*He sits down on a packing case and proceeds to rock the pram gently.*) Well, Frankie boy, I wonder what you're going to turn out like! You're not going to get any wrong ideas, see? That is, not if I have anything to do with it. . . . There's nobody here to interrupt us, so we can talk as man to man, can't we? There's not much to worry about really, so long as you remember one or two things always. The first is that life isn't all jam for anybody, and you've got to have trouble of some kind or another, whoever you are. But if you don't let it get you down, however bad it is, you won't go far wrong. . . . Another thing you'd better get into that little bullet head of yours

221

is that you belong to something that nobody can't ever break, however much they try. And they'll try all right— they're trying now. Not only people in other countries who want to do us in because they're sick of us ruling the roost —and you can't blame them at that!—but people here in England. People who have let 'emselves get soft and afraid. People who go on a lot about peace and good will and the ideals they believe in, but somehow don't seem to believe in 'em enough to think they're worth fighting for. . . . The trouble with the world is, Frankie, that there are too many ideals and too little horse sense. We're human beings, we are—all of us—and that's what people are liable to forget. Human beings don't like peace and good will and everybody loving everybody else. However much they may think they do, they don't really because they're not made like that. Human beings like eating and drinking and loving and hating. They also like showing off, grabbing all they can, fighting for their rights, and bossing anybody who'll give 'em half a chance. You belong to a race that's been bossy for years and the reason it's held on as long as it has is that nine times out of ten it's behaved decently and treated people right. Just lately, I'll admit, we've been giving at the knees a bit and letting people down who trusted us and allowing noisy little men to bully us with a lot of guns and bombs and aeroplanes. But don't worry—that won't last— the people themselves, the ordinary people like you and me, know something better than all the fussy old politicians put together—we know what we belong to, where we come from, and where we're going. We may not know it with our brains, but we know it with our roots. And we know another thing, too, and it's this. We 'aven't lived and died and struggled all these hundreds of years to get decency and justice and freedom for ourselves without being prepared to fight fifty wars if need be—to keep 'em.

(ETHEL *comes in.*)

ETHEL

What in the world are you doing? Talking to yourself?

FRANK

I wasn't talking to myself—I was talking to Frankie.

ETHEL

Well, I'm sure I hope he enjoyed it.

FRANK

He's stopped dribbling, anyhow!

ETHEL

Come on in—supper's ready. You'd better close the windows, he might get a chill.

(ETHEL *goes out.* FRANK *closes the windows and goes back to the pram.*)

FRANK

So long, son. . . .

(*He goes out as the*

CURTAIN FALLS.)